TRUST
Signals

SCOTT BARADELL

TRUST
Signals

Brand Building in a Post-Truth World

LIONCREST
PUBLISHING

Trust Signals
Brand Building in a Post-Truth World

ISBN 978-1-5445-2782-6 Hardcover
      978-1-5445-2780-2 Paperback
      978-1-5445-2781-9 Ebook
      978-1-5445-3662-0 Audiobook

To Kenji Miyazawa,

whose words of encouragement I taped

on the wall when things were at their worst.

And to Maria, who made

everything better.

Contents

Acknowledgments

I would like to express thanks to my families at work and home for their help and support during this project. First and foremost, I am grateful to my wife, Maria, and my children, Juliet, Benjamin, Jack, Christopher, and Margaret, who provided consistent love and support over the course of this challenging but worthwhile journey.

I'd like to thank Idea Grove's president and chief operating officer, John Lacy, and longtime agency leaders Katie Long, Liz Cies, Megan Chesterton, Jarrett Rush, Brittany McLaughlin, and Les Worley, who have guided the agency so well during this time.

Thanks also to Cecil Cross, Alexis Diehl, Laurie Lane, Talissa Beall, Carlee Ortiz, Stephanie Jatnieks, Christina Davies, Taylor Hering, Rose Jun, Julia Jarvis, Lauren Wyder, Mary Brynn Milburn, Chris Pham, Jilianne Scamperle, Mandi Sadler, and Lindsay Bell, who performed research and contributed content to the book. I also appreciate the talents and patience of Tucker Max, Lisa Caskey, Teresa Muniz, and the entire team at Scribe Media and Lioncrest.

Finally, I'd like to thank my bosses, employees, clients, peers, and mentors over the years who inspired this work and its contents. Please note that I have protected identities in instances where my words might be interpreted as unflattering. The conversation with "David," in particular, is a composite of various discussions with various colleagues at various breakfasts featuring runny eggs over the years.

Introduction

The Dirty Little Secret about PR

As a longtime PR guy, I'd like to start by speaking to others in my profession. Because while *Trust Signals* provides practical advice for all marketers and business owners, I wrote this book specifically to advance the field of public relations.

The Public Relations Society of America (PRSA) defines PR as:

> a strategic communication process that builds mutually beneficial relationships between organizations and their publics. ("About Public Relations")

In common practice, however, the definition of PR is much narrower than that.

Simply put, the job of most PR professionals has been to help brands procure media coverage and to influence the tone of that coverage—to place positive stories in the news. PR professionals have understood this definition to be a limiting one for years, but still haven't managed to come up with anything better.

I've heard many well-meaning PR people attempt to refute this reality, twisting themselves into rhetorical pretzels in the process. But the fact remains that to the majority of brand executives—particularly at midsize companies and smaller—PR *is* media relations.

Nothing more, nothing less.

The rest of what most integrated PR agencies do today is better known to clients by a different term: *marketing*.

Which, of course, raises the question: "What's the difference between PR and marketing, anyway?" And does it even matter?

THE DIFFERENCE BETWEEN PR AND MARKETING

I would argue there is a difference, and it does matter—because if a PR practitioner or PR firm doesn't know what they are uniquely suited to do relative to marketers, or why they exist relative to marketing agencies, there's no point in having a profession that calls itself "PR" in the first place, is there?

Without a clear definition and purpose, every PR person is a marketing person, and every PR agency is a marketing agency. And the only distinction in the minds of clients is that the marketing agency that calls itself a "PR firm" is probably a little better at media relations—and a little worse at everything else.

Many business executives today would describe PR as subordinate to marketing—a tool in the marketer's toolkit. In the same way that the majority of execs view PR's primary role as media relations, most also see PR as just another arrow in the marketing quiver, no different from SEO or display advertising or media buying.

That's not how public relations professionals have traditionally viewed themselves, however.

Historically, PR practitioners have regarded PR as not merely a *tool* of marketing, but the *equal* of marketing as a strategic discipline and management function.

Public relations, its proponents have argued, is the rightful keeper of corporate identity and brand reputation. The PR function, in fact, should lead overall brand communications—not only to customers, but to investors, employees, partners, community activists, and the public at large.

As a writer for PRSA's (2015) *PRsay* blog put it:

> Marketing addresses consumers of a product or service. Public relations is the strategic function that addresses all of an organization's key constituencies.

That's a much more ambitious vision than chasing down reporters for media coverage, isn't it?

A DIMINISHED PROFESSION

So what happened?

Why does the marketing department control the brand and budget for the vast majority of businesses?

Why does the organization's PR leader typically report to the CMO or vice president of marketing, when in the past it was more common to report directly to the CEO—and when according to industry surveys, more than 70 percent of PR leaders *still* say they should report to the CEO?

Why isn't the PR function entrusted with responsibility for building, growing, and protecting the corporate brand?

The answer is that PR practitioners have diminished their own profession—mostly by sins of omission. They haven't kept up with the times, redefined their role, or expanded their relevance in the face of change.

IVY LEE VERSUS EDWARD BERNAYS:
PR CHOOSES THE WRONG HORSE

To understand how PR got here, let's take a look back at the history of public relations in the United States.

In the first half of the twentieth century, PR was faced with two fundamentally different paths to follow. These approaches were championed by two men who have been called the "fathers" of PR: Edward Bernays and Ivy Lee.

Lee and Bernays

Lee was a former journalist who took a straightforward approach to helping his clients by building relationships with the media. Bernays—whose uncle was Sigmund Freud, the founder of psychoanalysis—had more ambitious goals for public relations. He wanted to elevate it to the status of a true profession, like law or medicine, built on the science of understanding what makes people tick.

Lee's most famous contribution to the profession was his "Declaration of Principles," in which he promised journalists that his goal was to provide them with accurate information, and not to manipulate facts to his client's advantage.

Lee's declaration proclaimed:

> We aim to supply news; this is not an advertising agency. Further details on any subject treated will be supplied promptly, and any editor will be assisted most carefully in verifying directly any statement of fact. (Russell and Bishop 2009)

Bernays, on the other hand, took pride in using audience research and social psychology to influence behavior. He called it "engineering consent" and considered it critical to democracy, having served with the US Committee on Public Information to build support for American participation in World War I.

As he explained in his 1928 book, *Propaganda*:

> Modern business must have its finger continuously on the public pulse. The voice of the people expresses the mind of the people...composed of inherited prejudices and symbols and cliches and verbal formulas... (Bernays)

Bernays aimed for PR practitioners to become experts in understanding these "prejudices and symbols and cliches and verbal formulas" to better connect with the audiences they sought to influence.

The PR industry ultimately took the simpler, less controversial path of Lee, led by organizations such as the PRSA, which was founded in 1947 and remains the industry's top professional association. By and large, PR practitioners have tethered their fate—and their value as professionals—to the news media ever since.

The emergence and explosive growth of US mass media following World War II led to a parallel boom in PR. The future of PR seemed assured—so long as the mainstream news media continued to dominate the public consciousness, serving as gatekeepers for brand awareness and arbiters for brand trust.

Unfortunately, as traditional media have fragmented and lost influence over time, public relations has struggled along with it.

A VICIOUS CYCLE

"Facts are facts," as old-school journalists like to say.

And the facts are these:

In 2008, there were 115,000 total newsroom employees—reporters, editors, photographers, and videographers—across newspapers, TV, radio, and online publishers. By 2020, according to a 2021 Pew Research Center analysis, that number had dropped to 85,000, a loss of 30,000 jobs (Walker 2021).

That's a 26 percent decline in a little more than a decade. It's basic economics: in inflation-adjusted dollars, ad revenues for the news media have been in a constant state of decline for forty years.

That means fewer journalists are around to cover stories—which in turn means PR professionals have to work harder, and spend more time than ever, to get their attention.

And when coverage is achieved, it typically attracts fewer readers or viewers and wields less influence than before—the product of splintered audiences and scattered information sources.

It's a vicious cycle.

WHERE DO WE GO FROM HERE?
BACK TO THE FUTURE

The question that really troubles me, and that should be of concern to everyone in the public relations business, is this:

When you start extending the definition of PR beyond media relations, what is truly unique to PR?

If you look closely at the way many public relations firms describe themselves today, it's like you're staring at the hole in a doughnut.

Some global agencies make a big deal of calling themselves "progressive PR firms." Or they portray themselves as integrated agencies that are "earned first"—referring to earning media exposure through PR rather than buying it through ads.

But these definitions fail to resonate. They don't meaningfully differentiate between what is PR and what isn't—and they don't explain why clients should care about the distinction.

So, where do PR practitioners go from here?

Suffice it to say that PR cannot remain so tightly anchored to the news media. That's why I would argue that, for inspiration, the profession should look not to the ideas of Lee, but to those of Bernays.

START WITH THE WHY, NOT THE HOW

The Bernays path—one focused less on the "how" of tactics and more on the "why" of strategy—is the better one for PR's future.

I'm not suggesting diving into some of the darker arts of psychological manipulation advocated by Bernays. His legacy is far from untarnished. But I do believe PR professionals should take a step back from media relations to ask themselves this question:

What is the business goal of media coverage?

Achieving this business goal, after all, is what's most important to brands. It's certainly what matters to the clients of PR agencies like mine.

What, then, is the business goal of media coverage? Most PR clients would tell you it is visibility. But that's only what they *think* they want. I would argue it's not what they *actually* want.

If PR clients simply wanted visibility—if they just wanted to raise brand awareness—it would be more cost-effective for them to buy ads to follow their target audiences around wherever they went online, wouldn't it?

Of course it would.

THE WHY IS TRUST

What PR clients are really seeking is credibility. They are seeking authority. They are seeking third-party validation.

Ultimately, they are seeking one thing above all else:

Trust.

Brands need to be trusted in the marketplace, or they won't be able to grow.

Traditionally, PR firms have leveraged third-party validation from the news media to earn trust for their clients. But media coverage alone isn't enough anymore. In fact, it's far from enough.

Today's brands must gain trust in other ways.

A NEW DEFINITION FOR PR: SECURING TRUST AT SCALE

Let's go back to the PRSA definition of public relations I referenced at the outset of this introduction, because it deserves another look.

To be clear, I am a longtime member and advocate of the PRSA. I have spoken at its events, attended its conferences, judged its competitions, and held its Accredited in Public Relations (APR) credential for more than two decades.

I respect the care PRSA takes to update the definition periodically. Most recently, in 2012, the organization reached out to thousands of members, solicited hundreds of suggestions, and took a vote before announcing the new official definition.

As we learned earlier in this introduction, it reads as follows:

Public relations is a strategic communication process that builds mutually beneficial relationships between organizations and their publics.

This description has its merits. It doesn't anchor the profession to the media or subordinate it to the marketing function.

But it's missing something important: an objective. A CEO or CMO has never asked me to help build "mutually beneficial relationships." That's a means—but to what end?

To answer this question, I've created an alternative definition of PR. It's short and to the point:

PR is the art of securing trust at scale.

While that's a very specific objective, it opens up limitless possibilities for PR professionals to help brands achieve that goal.

For starters, PR practitioners should consider their first responsibility to serve as trust experts and advocates—to be the *keepers of trust* for brands. PR practitioners are well-suited to this role, and it certainly lifts PR to the status of strategic discipline and management function.

How should PR practitioners assert themselves in this role? In any number of ways, many of which are outlined in this book.

For example, in the same way that marketers create buyer personas, PR practitioners can create *trust profiles* for their clients' target audiences to better understand the "prejudices, symbols, cliches, and verbal formulas" that influence trust.

Based on these profiles, PR pros can then master and deploy an evolving set of practices—which I describe as *trust signals*—to secure audience trust.

TRUST SIGNALS: BUILDING, GROWING, AND PROTECTING BRANDS

Trust Signals is all about the tools and tactics that businesses can use to build, grow, and protect their brands. And while marketers and business owners can deploy the practices outlined in this book, my belief is that this work is uniquely suited to PR practitioners— who have always focused on earning credibility rather than selling products.

PR firms and corporate communications departments don't need to be all things to all people. They must simply become better than any other type of agency or function at understanding what makes buyers, and other audiences, *trust*.

If PR leaders truly want to elevate their profession—if they want to guide corporate identity, lead brand strategy, and report to the CEO again—that's the path for doing it.

This book will show you how.

PART 1

Understanding
Trust Signals

CHAPTER 1

The Breakfast Meeting

→ PR campaigns that focus narrowly on media coverage often
fail to meet the expectations of brands.

→ Today's audiences look to a wide variety of information
sources, which all must be factored into campaigns.

→ PR practitioners must deploy an evolving set of tools to
achieve the ultimate goal of building brand trust.

I hadn't heard from my friend David in years. But when my former colleague reached out over LinkedIn to ask for a breakfast meeting at a nearby diner, I accepted the invitation right away.

I liked David and enjoyed sharing war stories about our days together in the corporate world at a wireless communications company. David was a senior network engineer whom I frequently offered up for interviews with the news media.

When it came to media interviews, David was a natural. He made my job easier because he could discuss telecommunications in engaging language that even the most technology-challenged reporters could understand.

"Oh, I get it," they would always say.

That was music to my ears, because it inevitably led to better, longer, and more sympathetic stories about our company.

The coverage was a feather in my cap and great personal branding for David.

A NEW JOB—AND A DAUNTING CHALLENGE

The sky in downtown Dallas was clear and crystal blue that morning as I walked into the restaurant. David spotted me immediately and stood up and waved from a corner booth.

"Hey! It's good to see you," he said.

We shook hands, then slid into our respective sides of the booth to order our food and talk.

I quickly learned that the visibility David had achieved through his role as a thought leader had helped him secure a position as CEO with a promising mobile commerce startup that had received more than ten million dollars the previous year in VC funding. David was in his third week on the job.

"That's very exciting, David," I said. "How is business going? Are you doing well?"

"Yes and no," David told me. "Securing that funding was amazing for a bootstrapped startup that had just gotten off the ground. And the technology is sound. But the company has only landed a handful of customers, and they just haven't been able to leverage their financial resources to accelerate their growth as yet.

"That's why the investors brought me in," he continued. "They want someone who understands the technology and can communicate it in a compelling, credible way, and I've earned a reputation for that."

"Yes, you have," I said. "So what's your next move? How can I help?"

"I'm getting to that," he said with a smile. "Shortly after the founder got funding, he brought in a big PR firm to get the word out. He thought his company had built a better mousetrap, and he wanted the world to know about it. He expected the sales to follow.

"Unfortunately, a year later, it hasn't worked out that way. That's why he was asked to step aside as CEO."

ROSY PIE CHARTS, SAD REALITY

I asked David what kind of results his new company had seen from its investment in PR.

He told me that, in doing his research before joining the startup, he had found articles in *TechCrunch*, *Fast Company*, *Forbes*, and a number of industry trade publications.

Then, a few days after he started as CEO, the PR agency came to his office to make a presentation. They showed him a pie chart indicating the company had increased its share of voice relative to its competitors. They were now receiving 20 percent more industry coverage than when the engagement started.

"The agency expressed satisfaction with this result. But it didn't really add up to much in terms of impact for us—certainly not what the founder was hoping for," David said.

"What specific impact was the founder hoping for?" I asked.

"He wanted it to open doors for us, and it didn't," David shrugged. "No one really saw or mentioned the coverage. No one recognized our name when we emailed or called them.

"Traffic to the website went up briefly when the agency put out a press release, but then it would flatten out again. We've seen no sustained lift in people finding out about us or wanting to learn more."

David then told me he believed the founder hired the wrong agency; he wanted to work with my agency instead.

"I know PR can make a big difference, because it did when we worked together before. I want you to get us on the map. I want media coverage that will help our salespeople get a better response rate."

LOWERING MY FORK—AND THE BOOM

I realized, at this point, that my eggs were so runny that they had made my plate look like a yolk-splattered crime scene. So I put down my fork and decided to stick to the coffee.

I took a long sip before responding.

"PR has changed, David. What we did back when we worked together doesn't work now."

"I'm not sure I understand," he replied. "It's all about hustling to get media coverage, right? Coming up with story ideas, figuring out the right media, building relationships to get visibility—isn't that the whole point of the job?"

"It's fair to say it *used to be* the whole point of the job. And many agencies still operate that way—the agency you just fired, for example," I said.

"But the problem is not that the agency isn't good at what they do; it's that they are doing the wrong things."

David's complaints are all too common among dissatisfied clients. They truly believe the agency just needs to "hustle" harder to get results.

But the truth is, PR practitioners who fail their clients are rarely incompetent or lazy. In fact, in many cases they are working harder than ever.

The problem is that they are still doing what worked five or ten years ago—and not what works today.

THE INCREDIBLE SHRINKING GATEKEEPER

David's interest was piqued, and he asked to hear more. I gathered my thoughts before continuing.

"Look, this pains me to say, David. I started my career as a newspaper reporter. I believe in journalism. But the fact is it used to be that if you were in a front-page story in *The Dallas Morning News*, that had a powerful, immediate impact," I said.

"Think about it. The paper carrier would throw that big Sunday newspaper on your front porch, you'd pick it up, and the whole world would seemingly know you were on the front page.

"Now, who knows the difference between a 'front-page story' and any other story on the paper's website? And who reads it, anyway?"

I then shared a startling—and sobering—fact about our home-town newspaper. The paid circulation of *The Dallas Morning News* is *less than a third* of what it was two decades ago; that includes both print and digital subscribers. This is during a time period when the population of the Dallas/Fort Worth area is booming—growing by *nearly a third*, with new transplants from California and elsewhere arriving daily.

A CASE OF DIMINISHING RETURNS

It's a classic case of diminishing returns, I explained. And it's not just true for newspapers—it applies to virtually all media outlets targeting broad-based audiences.

The cycle we're experiencing is this:

- Fewer journalists are around to cover stories, so...
- PR people have to work harder and spend more time to get journalists' attention, but...
- when a high-profile outlet finally does cover you, it's seen by fewer people, and...
- it's far less likely your intended audience will ever see the coverage amid today's endless sea of information sources.

David had come upon media coverage about his new employer during the interview process, but only because he had searched for the company by name. And while PR firms can use paid media, such as retargeting ads, to better expose coverage to target audiences, many agencies simply don't consider this part of their jobs.

"That's why the work that other PR agency did for you had so little impact," I told David. "They thought their job began and ended with getting publicity, when today that is only one piece of a much larger puzzle."

UNLIMITED PAGES, SMALL AUDIENCES

David frowned for a moment—then his eyes lit up.

"But some mainstream media sites seem to be doing really well," he said. "*Forbes*, for example. They sent me a media kit and it said they reached more than 100 million unique visitors per month. That's much bigger than their readership in the past, according to the media kit."

"That's true, but it's also a bit deceptive," I cautioned.

Traffic on the *Forbes* website is spread out over more than 1.5 million pages on the Forbes.com domain, so most stories get relatively few visitors—especially compared to the kind of audience an article in the print version of *Forbes* once commanded.

There is no limit to how much content you can publish on a website, so outlets like Forbes.com have decided that more pages are better for traffic. In order to achieve that, over the years they have recruited thousands of contributors to publish on their platform—often just for the privilege of saying they are published by *Forbes*.

THE ECONOMICS OF THE BYLINE

I told David that this never-ending demand for online content, combined with the lack of sufficient numbers of journalists to create it, has led to an explosion of so-called "bylined article" opportunities—chances for a brand to submit content with their CEO's name on the byline.

In the past, I explained, when a PR person pitched a story that a publication's editor liked, a reporter for the publication would be assigned to interview the company executive for ten minutes and then write a story. Now if the editor likes your idea, they're more likely to ask *you* to write the story. A ten-hour time commitment to write a 1,500-word article is a much bigger ask than a ten-minute interview.

David cradled his coffee cup in his hands. "Yes, a number of the placements the other PR firm got us were bylined articles in trade journals. Are you saying we *shouldn't* write articles for industry publications?"

"You should," I replied, "but you have to be selective. Most PR agencies aren't, because they grade themselves on the *number* of placements they achieve rather than the return they deliver. When the only tool you have is the media hammer, you'll pound on any nail you can to demonstrate your value to the client."

I explained that my agency has a checklist we run through before recommending a byline to a client. For example, we make sure the outlet is a Google News source, has industry credibility and a relevant audience, has high domain authority as measured by marketing-analytics companies (like Moz and Ahrefs), and will agree to link back to the client's website. We also make sure the client has something worthwhile to say to that publication's readers; otherwise, it's just not worth it.

The sad fact is, many of the bylined articles that PR firms get published today—often at great expense—quickly disappear into the bowels of the internet, never to be heard from again.

TAKING A HOLISTIC APPROACH TO TRUST

David paused for a moment. "So what's my best play then, given all these changes? Where does that leave you as an agency? And me as a potential client, for that matter?"

I smiled reassuringly.

"Well, I've spent most of breakfast giving you the bad news, so let me finally give you the good news. People are still reading and consuming information, including information about brands, companies, products—and thought leaders like you. They're just consuming it in different ways.

"I've watched these trends develop for a while, David—with increasing levels of frustration. I finally decided to stop focusing on media coverage for its own sake, and to start focusing on its ultimate objective. I decided to tackle that larger goal for my clients."

"So what is that larger goal?" David asked. "Awareness? Visibility?"

"No," I said. "Your goal is to achieve *brand trust*. Brand exposure is meaningless without trust. Without trust, nothing else you do with your marketing budget matters. You'll never be able to open those doors your founder wants you to open if you don't first build trust.

"Fortunately, there are many ways to secure brand trust today besides hounding journalists to write about you."

I asked the waitress for the check.

"Hey!" David objected. "Not so fast—I asked *you* to breakfast."

"That's OK," I smiled. "I have a feeling you're going to be a new client soon, so I'm writing this meal off as a business-development expense."

The next week, we were off and running on a PR program focused not on media coverage, but on securing trust at scale—by deploying *trust signals* to build, grow, and protect David's brand.

CHAPTER 2

Living—and Branding—
in a Post-Truth World

→ In a world without gatekeepers, the job of PR is to reach the
most valuable sources of truth for a brand's audience.

→ Influence is a continuum, starting with customer reviews
and progressing to mega-influencers and top-tier media.

→ Research is required to discover which sources inspire trust,
or distrust, in a brand's audience.

In 2016, Oxford Dictionaries named "post-truth" its Word of the Year. A Google search for the term today yields more than 2.5 million results.

The word was coined by writer Steve Tesich after the US government prohibited the news media from covering the 1991 Persian Gulf War except in carefully controlled press pools. In a piece in *The Nation*, Tesich lamented that the public had been fed only official, sanitized accounts of the conflict—and had barely protested (Kreitner 2016).

This was in sharp contrast to the Vietnam War, when American journalists roamed freely in Saigon and the Vietnamese countryside, recording and amplifying the trauma of that conflict.

Tesich's conclusion was this:

We came to equate truth with bad news and we didn't want bad news anymore, no matter how true…In a very fundamental way we, as a free people, have freely decided that we want to live in some post-truth world. (Kreitner 2016)

Tesich's analysis describes the fundamental challenge our public institutions and businesses face today. Because thanks to social media algorithms and competing media echo chambers, Americans *never* have to encounter bad news anymore—or at least not news that conflicts with their chosen point of view.

Oxford Dictionaries defines *post-truth* as "circumstances in which objective facts are less influential in shaping public opinion than appeals to emotion and personal belief" (Oxford Languages, n.d.). Ironically, however, in a post-truth world, even this definition is subject to debate because many people don't believe objective facts are "less influential." They believe they simply don't exist.

This reality is both a result of and reason for the decline of mainstream media gatekeepers, which I described in the opening chapters of this book. Audiences have fragmented and scattered across thousands of information sources that align with their interests and cater to what Edward Bernays called their preferred "prejudices and symbols and cliches and verbal formulas."

IN TRUMP WE TRUST

Use of the term "post-truth" by the media and public began climbing the charts on June 16, 2015—the day Donald Trump descended that golden escalator to announce his bid for the presidency.

Few topics are more divisive today than Trump. But while much of the reporting on Trump has focused on his controversial positions and brash rhetoric, I would argue that this is not what has created the huge chasm between Trump's supporters and his detractors.

The main issue was, and is, *truth*—specifically, different understandings of what's true and what's not.

The Washington Post claimed Trump made more than 30,000 false or misleading statements during his four years in office (Kessler, Rizzo, and Kelly 2021). A 2020 Pew Research Poll found that only 7 percent of Democrats considered Trump "honest." And yet, that same poll revealed that more than 70 percent of Republicans judged him to be truthful ("Public's Mood Turns Grim").

In fact, millions of Trump's fans believe that he is the most trustworthy leader we've ever had—or as political analyst Bruce Wolpe (2019) put it, "the most ruthlessly honest president of modern times."

WHY DO YOU SUPPORT DONALD TRUMP?

In July 2020, I wrote a post on the question-and-answer website Quora responding to the question, "Why do you support Donald Trump?" The answer earned hundreds of thousands of views and thousands of upvotes, with plaudits equally divided between liberals and conservatives. Here's that Quora answer.

I don't personally support Donald Trump, but I know many who do. Here's my take.

The other day, I was searching a thesaurus website for synonyms of "strategy." I was stunned by the words the site listed as its antonyms: "honesty" and "openness."

Hmm. What's that about?

The Oxford definition of "strategy" is simply "a plan of action or policy designed to achieve a major or overall aim."

Why does this suggest dishonesty or lack of openness?

I think it relates to the human instinct to associate spontaneity with candor, and deliberate planning with manipulative plotting.

Preparation as a Proxy for Dishonesty

I had a girlfriend once who broke up with me during an argument. One reason she gave for her decision was that I took too long to answer her questions.

"What?" I asked her.

She thought that when she asked me about our relationship, religion, or any other topic big or small, I should be at the ready with a response.

Unfortunately, that's not me. I like to be thoughtful when asked a question—so I tend to pause and prepare for a moment before saying anything.

In my ex-girlfriend's mind, I was plotting. I was coming up with the answer I wanted her to hear, rather than simply telling her the truth that should have been on the tip of my tongue.

"What does your crazy ex-girlfriend have to do with a discussion about strategy?" you might be asking.

Well, she actually wasn't so crazy. Many people think a person is more honest when they are less careful in their choice of words.

The Spur-of-the-Moment Magic of Trump

Even President Donald Trump's biggest supporters would be unlikely to label him a meticulous strategist. He exudes spontaneity in every sound bite, public appearance, and tweet.

And that's why millions of Americans believe he's the most honest US president—perhaps even politician, period—our country has ever seen, despite significant objective evidence to the contrary.

Americans who voted for Trump in 2016 were looking for the exact opposite of a classic politician.

An antonym, if you will.

After all, politicians have never been known for their spontaneity. They have been known for being calculating, judicious, crafty, cautious—*strategic*.

Historically, they have been trained to be all things to all people, while having views that perfectly coincide with their party's platform. Their carefully crafted sound bites—however acrobatic—have become increasingly alienating to voters.

When people see Trump, they see someone who is being himself, for good or ill.

He's himself, and despite enormous pressures—from his party, from the media, from everyone—he has refused to change. He has refused to apologize. He has doubled down on being *true to himself*.

That's why so many people trust him. To his supporters, the many small lies Trump is caught telling are nothing compared to his rare, unscripted consistency as a person.

His supporters don't love him *despite* his lack of careful strategy and deliberate communication. They love him *because* of it.

BRANDS IN A POST-TRUTH WORLD

The divide over Trump and truth gets to the essence of what "post-truth" means in practical terms today—for the media, the public, and brands.

If the same person can be both the "most honest" and "most dishonest" president in history, depending on the audience, what does this say about the importance of understanding which audiences your brand is targeting and how best to engage with them?

While post-truth is usually discussed in a political context, its implications for business are far-reaching and transformative. Every brand must have trust to succeed, and earning that trust requires third-party validation from media outlets and other sources of influence that buyers consider credible and authoritative.

That goal becomes harder to achieve in a post-truth world, when the sources of third-party validation themselves are not only more fragmented, but also less trusted.

The disappearance of shared sources of truth, such as media gatekeepers and civic institutions, means that a brand must carefully sift through a highly fragmented information landscape to cobble together a collection of sources that will have credibility for the brand's target audience.

FINDING THOSE WHO SPEAK YOUR TRUTH

The term "speak your truth" may not be an Oxford Dictionaries Word of the Year like "post-truth," but it has gained similar popularity in recent years.

Particularly for those who believe their voices haven't always been heard in mainstream culture, it's powerful phrasing. Unlike simply sharing an opinion or experience, stating your "truth" implies that others' understanding of the truth may be flawed or incomplete.

It also conveys an inarguable quality. Your opinion can be changed. Your experience can be enriched. Your "truth," however, is immutable.

We live in a world that is not only post-truth, but in which people speak their truths in places where they know they will find friendly audiences—social spheres where open disagreement can quickly lead to excommunication.

What does this have to do with brands? A lot.

THE LONG TAIL OF SPOKEN TRUTHS

Back in 2004, Chris Anderson of *Wired* magazine popularized the statistical term "long tail" for online marketers, explaining that in an era of unlimited web "shelf space," products that have a low sales volume could collectively earn a market share exceeding that of the comparatively few high-volume products, if the distribution channel were large enough ("The Long Tail").

At a time when Amazon was on course to overtake Walmart as the most powerful retailer in the world, it was hard to argue Anderson's point. Since that time, the long tail has emerged as a key consideration for marketing strategists in an environment of ever-increasing media fragmentation and niche marketing.

But this era of unlimited digital shelf space is relevant not only to product marketing; it applies to public discourse as well. Our "spoken truths" have a long tail, too.

That's why lesser-known social media influencers who barely earn a peep of attention on mainstream media, for example, can collectively drive greater results for a brand than the mainstream outlets that ignore them. These influencers have smaller followings, but impassioned ones that trust them because of their shared truths.

WHEN THE TINY NEWSLETTER BEATS
THE BIG NEWSPAPER

I recently spoke with a PR practitioner who told me that in working to drum up attendance for a local event, she had great difficulty securing stories in the local newspaper and business weekly. After much time and effort, she was finally able to score the placements— but after all was said and done, the event could track zero registrations to that coverage.

On the other hand, landing a mention in the email newsletter of a highly opinionated local influencer was a key driver of registrations and helped make the event a success. The reason is that, while small, the influencer's audience was more targeted and far more passionate about the event's subject matter. The influencer's audience also trusted that if he endorsed the event, it was worth their time and money.

And here's the kicker: my friend actually paid the influencer for the mention. It was not an "earned" placement; it was sponsored. But because the influencer's audience trusted his recommendations, whether he was paid to make them or not was irrelevant.

THE CONTINUUM OF INFLUENCE

Brands must recognize that in a world without gatekeepers influence is a continuum.

It begins, on the low end, with any customer who leaves a review of your company or product on an online-review site. While this individual reviewer might not have a recognized name, their review nevertheless has an influence on those who read it.

If that customer already has an established following on social media, their influence when saying something positive (or negative) about your business is that much greater. The greater the influencer's following, the larger their megaphone.

As influencers increase their name recognition and audience size, they progress on the continuum from nano-influencer all the way up to mega-influencer.

Influence Is a Continuum

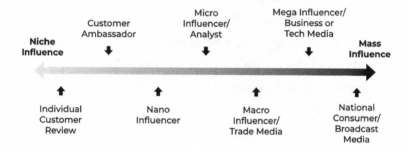

THE KARDASHIANS AND *THE NEW YORK TIMES*

You can think of mega-influencers as major media outlets, like *The New York Times*, and big celebrities, like the Kardashians.

The New York Times and the Kardashians are obviously very different sources of information, but both are highly trusted by certain segments of consumers. Your job as a marketer or PR professional is to identify the continuum of influence—from the individual customer to major media outlets—that are the most valuable sources of truth for your audience.

I should add that (while this point may make PR traditionalists blanch) it doesn't matter whether the influencer is paid or organic as long as they are transparent about brand sponsorships. Focus on whether an influencer has a real following and real credibility with that following—then, determine how well that following matches your audience.

DON'T READY, FIRE, AIM—DO YOUR RESEARCH

The range of options in a brand's continuum of influence should make evident the importance of primary research into the habits and beliefs of your buyers and other key audiences.

The playing field is far more complex and the stakes much higher than in the past. It's no longer sufficient to gather a group of executives in a conference room, whiteboard their opinions, and call it a day. You should perform quantitative and qualitative research that includes buyer personas as well as *trust profiles* that study your audience's sources of influence in detail. (We'll discuss trust profiles later in this book.)

During this research, your objective is to discover what sources inspire trust, as well as distrust, in your buyers and other audiences.

The answers may surprise you—and it's not something that should be left to guesswork or chance.

DO IT THE OLD WAY AT YOUR PERIL

Years ago, I began seeing the implications of a post-truth world on business. I had just scored a major *New York Times* feature opportunity for one of my agency's oil-and-gas clients.

In the past, this would have been a huge coup for our agency and our client. This time, the client's CEO—after originally accepting the interview—turned it down at the last minute because "nobody trusts the *Times* anymore."

Of course, it wasn't true that nobody trusted *The New York Times*. But it was true that it had lost credibility with many in the energy industry, including this client's own customers. The company's CEO had actually been talked out of the interview after conversations with his own employees and customers.

For them, *The Wall Street Journal*, Fox Business Network, or even the local newspaper had become a more trusted source of influence.

I hadn't done my research before securing this placement, and it cost me. That *New York Times* reporter never wanted to hear from me again.

JUST DO IT—WITH AUDIENCE DATA

Remember the controversy in 2018 when Nike made civil-rights activist and former NFL star Colin Kaepernick one of the faces of its thirtieth anniversary "Just Do It" campaign? Almost immediately, a #BoycottNike hashtag began trending on Twitter, and conservative media personalities lambasted the brand for choosing Kaepernick as a spokesperson.

And yet, Nike's sales and stock skyrocketed.

This result did not come as a surprise to Nike. Based on audience data, the company knew the association with Kaepernick would build trust and resonate with its core customer base, especially millennial and Generation Z men.

For another brand, an association with the same athlete might have been disastrous. For Nike, it was pure gold—because Kaepernick was a perfect fit in the brand's continuum of influence.

CHAPTER 3

The Eternal Power of Trust Signals

→ Trust signals are evidence points that inspire confidence in a brand online.

→ While the term is most closely associated with ecommerce stores, it applies to all brands today.

→ A breadcrumb trail of trust signals can accelerate every aspect of a brand's marketing funnel.

Since the construction of the Pharos of Alexandria, a three-hundred-foot lighthouse on the Egyptian Nile recognized as one of the Seven Wonders of the Ancient World, lighthouses have stood for safe harbor.

Because lighthouses are built to guide sailors through dangerous storms and turbulent waters in the dark of night, it's no wonder they have emerged as an enduring symbol of trust—as well as strength, hope, and for followers of the Christian faith, salvation.

The wood-burning flames of that ancient Egyptian structure, predecessors to beacons powered by whale oil, kerosene, and electric light that would emanate reassuringly from lighthouses for the next two thousand years, were one of the original *trust signals*.

WHAT IS A TRUST SIGNAL?

Trust signals can be found almost everywhere today, if you know where to look for them.

Consider your purchase of this book, for example.

Let's say you came across this title in a bookstore or on Amazon. You found the topic intriguing—but you've never heard of the author.

I'm not exactly famous, after all.

Before you buy the book, a question will inevitably cross your mind:

Can I trust this person—Scott Baradell?

Specifically, you want to know if you can trust that I have produced a work worth buying and spending your time on.

I, in turn, have attempted to prove my trustworthiness to you on the book jacket and online, by producing:

- an accomplished and relevant biography,
- glowing praise from well-known authors and respected authorities,
- five-star reviews on Amazon,
- acclaim on social media by people you might follow, and
- coverage in media outlets you know and respect.

These techniques to win your trust are all examples of trust signals. While they may occur naturally—earning positive reviews for writing a great book, for example—they should never be left to chance.

And they are no different from the flames of the Pharos of Alexandria in their ultimate intent: to guide those unsure about a path to take or decision to make.

Trust signals are the points of evidence that new authors, and all of us, use to win one another's trust.

We don't often think about it, but we spend our whole lives disseminating and processing trust signals:

- We seek out realtors, inspectors, and school-district ratings before deciding to buy a house—then we show the lender evidence we can be trusted to pay the mortgage.
- We scrutinize Glassdoor reviews to find a job we want— then we pack our resumes with credentials and accomplishments to win the offer.
- We stalk our would-be soulmates on social media and run Google background checks before venturing on a date—then we plaster our Instagram accounts with pictures that make us look like a good catch.

What trust signals do you seek out in others—whether it's to make a purchase, accept a job offer, or decide to marry someone?

What signals do you send?

Becoming conscious of these signals is an important step to becoming proficient at building trust, in business and life.

TRUST SIGNALS IN THE BUSINESS WORLD

In business, I define trust signals broadly, as anything that inspires confidence in your brand in the mind of your customers, employees, investors, and the general public.

Trust signals can be planned or unplanned, organic or paid, direct or subliminal. They are vital to every business: large or small, B2C or B2B, in every country and industry.

When a customer trusts your product or service, they are more likely to buy from you.

If they don't trust you, nothing else matters.

The term "trust signals" came into common parlance in the early days of internet commerce. Its definition was narrower then.

In a March 2000 article in the *Journal of Computer-Mediated Communication* titled, "The Role of Intermediaries in the Development of Trust on the WWW: The Use and Prominence of Trusted Third Parties and Privacy Statements," authors Jonathan W. Palmer, Joseph P. Bailey, and Samer Faraj make the case that for ecommerce to achieve its growth potential, "developing trust between suppliers and consumers is critical" ("The Role of Intermediaries in the Development of Trust on the WWW: The Use and Prominence of Trusted Third Parties and Privacy Statements").

The article describes the importance of displaying trust signals—in the form of endorsement seals from organizations such as the

Better Business Bureau and TRUSTe (now TrustArc)—to conversion rates on ecommerce websites.

To this day, most articles covering trust signals are still written with ecommerce marketers and SEO practitioners in mind.

Search for "trust signals" on Google and the following results turn up:

- "Your Ecommerce Site Will Die Without These 3 Trust Signals"
- "12 Trust Signals to Boost Your Conversion Rate"
- "10 Important Trust Signals for an Ecommerce Business"
- "5 Trust Signals to Boost Conversions for Your eCommerce Business"
- "Eight Trust Signals Every E-Commerce Site Needs"

Google Images results show thousands of images of trust seals that companies place on their sites to make buyers more comfortable making a purchase.

Indeed, these are all examples of trust signals.

But I would argue that to view the trust signal as simply a collection of badges to make people feel comfortable buying a product from your website is too limited a definition.

Today, not just ecommerce but *all* commerce is largely conducted online, thanks to the ascendancy of inbound marketing. Much of our lives are lived digitally, for that matter.

BUILDING BREADCRUMB PATHS TO TRUST

As I stated in this book's introduction I define PR as *the art of securing trust at scale.*

As such, trust signals are the tools that should fill up every PR professional's toolkit. A modern public relations agency should be able to help its clients build a path of credibility—*breadcrumbs of trust*—that accelerates every aspect of the marketing funnel.

Trust signals aren't just the seals and badges that convert website visitors. They're the evidence points consumers use to decide which websites to visit in the first place.

These evidence points might include customer reviews on review sites, featured coverage in the business press, and the endorsements of social media influencers.

All of these signals combine to drive buyers toward (or away from) your brand.

GOOGLE E-A-TS UP TRUST

Trust signals are important to Google as well. Virtually every trust signal is a ranking factor in determining your site's search position.

That's why SEO professionals and software have used names like Trust Flow, TrustRank, and MozTrust to describe what they do. They know that Google is trying to determine the trustworthiness of your site, just like potential customers.

This is particularly important to Google because it is more than a search engine—it is the most powerful media company in the world. And it has a long history of battling black-hat marketers who attempt to game Google to outrank better content. That reduces the quality of results, which has made these SEO outlaws Public Enemy No. 1 for the search giant.

In 2014 Google introduced the E-A-T formula for evaluating website page quality, an acronym for *expertise, authoritativeness,* and *trustworthiness.* This formula has only grown in importance in the years since. In its most recent Search Quality Evaluator Guidelines, Google (2022) references E-A-T more than 130 times.

While I respect the formula's sentiment, I might argue that it's a bit redundant. Expertise and authority, after all, are two of the main signals of trustworthiness.

What Google is really saying is that it is looking for signs that your website can be trusted based on its subject matter and how other websites covering the same topic view you. This is demonstrated when those other sites mention your brand or link to you. Google also studies traffic and usage data to determine which sites best serve their visitors.

TRUST SIGNALS IN A POST-TRUTH WORLD

Like everything today, *post-truth* means different things to different people. For the purposes of this book, post-truth is simply an acknowledgment that there has been a breakdown in *shared sources of truth* (such as the mainstream media, government, and Big Tech), as well as the concept of objective truth.

Importantly, post-truth doesn't equate to post-trust. It doesn't mean there is less trust, or less of a need for trust, than in the past. I specifically take issue with those who use Stephen Covey's term "low-trust world" to describe our current environment.

Indeed, I would argue that trust is immutable. We can't live our lives without it—at least not in a satisfying way.

Who and what we trust, on the other hand, can vary widely. In what some would call a "low-trust" world, we may trust the government or the mainstream media less, but our friends and family more.

The post-truth era has changed *who* we trust, *how* we trust, and *what* makes us trust. That's why understanding our customers and other audiences, and signaling our trustworthiness to them, is so important.

THE FRAGMENTATION OF TRUST

When people say we live in an era when people no longer trust each other, what they really mean is that we live in an era of *trust fragmentation*, because there are very few institutions the vast majority of Americans trust as part of a shared cultural identity.

In the last chapter, I told the story of an energy-company CEO who refused an interview with *The New York Times* because he didn't trust it to represent his company accurately—or to reach the audience that mattered to him. In his mind, a story in the *Times* would be unlikely to serve as a useful trust signal for his brand.

Trust fragmentation has been happening in the United States for decades—occurring notably in the traumatic, divisive 1960s. As far back as 1979, President Jimmy Carter famously bemoaned Americans' "growing disrespect for government and for churches and for schools, the news media, and other institutions." Over the past forty years, this trend has only accelerated.

But this fragmentation makes the people and organizations we *do* trust even *more* important to our identity and happiness, not less.

To return to the example of Donald Trump, one reason the former president inspires such an extreme level of devotion in his followers is that they share an extreme *lack* of trust in institutions like the mainstream media, academia, the scientific community, and global organizations like the United Nations and NATO.

THE TRUST SIGNAL MULTIVERSE

We're not in a low-trust world, in other words. We're in a trust *multiverse.*

Not to be confused with the metaverse hyped by Mark Zuckerberg and others, the multiverse is a hypothetical concept that most of us know about not from a graduate-level physics class, but from reading comic books and watching superhero movies—like Marvel's 2022 hit *Dr. Strange in the Multiverse of Madness.*

Basically, it's the idea that there are alternate, parallel, or even infinite universes rather than just our own.

To people in one universe, for example, the DC superhero Flash is a guy named Barry Allen wearing a red suit with a lightning bolt on the chest. But to people in a parallel universe, the Flash is Jay Garrick, the fellow with the silver kettle helmet.

And in *your* trust universe, people might believe what they hear on CNN. But in an alternate trust universe, Fox News might be gospel.

This isn't just about politics—although brands are increasingly expected to take a stand on political and social issues today.

Politics is only one dimension of the trust multiverse. Consumers, like voters, are eschewing traditional gatekeepers in favor of an ever-expanding range of sources of "truth."

An infinite array of trust signals.

That's why it's so important for every brand to know its customers well enough to understand which signals will most effectively earn their trust.

EXPLORING THE THREE TYPES OF ONLINE TRUST SIGNALS

In current digital marketing parlance, a trust signal can fall into three major categories:

1. **Website trust signals** that encourage visitors to complete a purchase or take an action
2. **Inbound trust signals** that drive visitors to your website via inbound marketing
3. **SEO trust signals** that visitors might not notice, but that Google uses to rank you in search

The next four chapters cover a comprehensive list of trust signals in each of these categories. Because there are so many website trust signals, I've broken them into two chapters, the first covering trust seals and the second covering the wide range of other signals your website can send.

From ancient Egyptian lighthouses to the endorsements on this book's dust jacket, trust signals have always been with us, and are all around us today.

You just need to know where to look—and how to use them to your advantage.

CHAPTER 4

Trust Seals—
From Medieval Kings
to Ecommerce

→ A trust seal is any website emblem, badge, or icon designed to quickly establish trust with visitors.

→ Trust seals deliver five key assurances: privacy, security, legitimacy, endorsement, and status.

→ The Better Business Bureau and TRUSTe badges are two of the oldest and most enduring trust seals.

S igned, sealed, and delivered.
    Seal of approval.
Sealed their fate.
Seal the deal.
Sealed with a kiss.
My lips are sealed.

These popular idioms derive from a common origin: the design stamped on wax known as a "seal" in English usage, beginning in the Middle Ages.

When you consider the wax seal today, you may think of decorative attachments to wedding invitations or special gifts. But the wax seal has borne far greater responsibility over the course of its fascinating one-thousand-plus-year history.

Wax seals have lessons to teach about trust, the importance of its tangible symbols, and their enduring role in business and in life.

As you'll learn in this chapter, there is a direct through line from the sealed writs of Medieval kings to the *trust seals* that began appearing on ecommerce websites in the late 1990s—and that are a pervasive online presence today.

KING JOHN'S LASTING CONTRIBUTION TO TRUST

In the thousand-year history of the British monarchy there is only one King John; he ruled from 1199 to 1216. The name was spoiled for future kings by John's reputation for being both cruel and cowardly —a combination that earned him the nickname "Softsword."

But one contribution of King John has endured—the impression of his seal in beeswax to affirm one of the most important documents in Western history, the Magna Carta.

In the Middle Ages, wax seals came into common use among

royals, bishops, and government officials to authenticate official documents. By the latter part of the thirteenth century, all levels of European society—from patricians to peasants—were using seals, both for business purposes and personal messages.

Over time, wax seals came to forge powerful associations with many aspects of trust, assuring privacy, security, legitimacy, endorsement, and status.

FIVE ASSURANCES DELIVERED BY WAX SEALS

Let's take a closer look at these five assurances:

#1: Privacy

When an envelope was sealed by wax, whether bearing a message of business or romance, it communicated that it was meant for the recipient's eyes only.

#2: Security

In addition to conveying that a message was private, the wax seal served as a practical method of security, indicating the missive had not been seen by others. A broken seal meant broken trust.

#3: Legitimacy

Legitimacy is validity as determined by the government or other authorizing organization. Wax seals stamped by such organizations established legitimacy.

#4: Endorsement

A step above legitimacy is endorsement, when a seal explicitly conveys approval or support. King John's seal on the Magna Carta established his endorsement of the agreement.

#5: Status

Powerful people typically pressed wax seals with a specially made signet ring, a symbol of status. High-ranking members of the church or government might require a visitor to kiss their signet to show their allegiance. When the signet's owner died, the ring would be destroyed to prevent forgeries.

FAST-FORWARD TO TRUST SEALS

Fast-forward to the present day and you'll find the more things change, the more they stay the same. In the internet age, trust seals —a direct descendant of the wax seal in etymology as well as meaning—have come to fill a key role in establishing trust in online commerce.

A trust seal can be defined as any emblem, badge, symbol, or icon intended to quickly establish trust with prospective customers and other audiences online.

In the early days of internet commerce, retailers realized that many consumers were skeptical of making purchases or sharing their credit-card information. Trust seals helped to reassure customers and remove friction from the buying process.

As the *Journal of Computer-Mediated Communication* put it in March 2000:

> Developing trust between suppliers and consumers is critical for the continued growth of Internet commerce...By using Trusted Third Parties (TTPs) and privacy statements, Internet retailers can help assuage some of consumers' concerns about the Internet. (Palmer, Bailey, and Faraj)

The TTPs were represented by seals from organizations such as the Better Business Bureau and TRUSTe, which emerged as the first widely used trust badges in the late 1990s.

The use and variety of trust seals on the web have expanded dramatically over the past two decades. To this day, research shows that trust seals on ecommerce sites can cut cart abandonment in half.

And such badges aren't just for online merchants anymore. Any brand can benefit from the instant social proof that trust seals can provide.

In ecommerce, trust seals are most visible during the checkout process, but many sites today use them on their home page, product pages, and *About Us* pages as well.

Let's take a closer look at the original trust badges—the Better Business Bureau and TRUSTe seals—which are still alive and kicking today.

The Better Business Bureau Seal

The Better Business Bureau (BBB) has been a symbol of trust not only since the early days of ecommerce, but dating back to the era of teletypes and horses and buggies.

In 1912, the organization emerged to help businesses respond to a crisis in public trust, when exaggerated advertising claims were the subject of high-profile lawsuits by the US government against the Coca-Cola Company and others.

More than a century later, the BBB is still relevant. Whereas retail storefronts in the pre-internet world proudly displayed the BBB logo in their shop windows, today about four hundred thousand accredited businesses worldwide display the trust seal on their websites.

Beyond those accredited companies, more than 6.2 million businesses have profiles at BBB.org, which receives 220 million website visits annually (BBB Serving the Heart of Texas 2021; Better Business Bureau, n.d.). Visitors use the site to search for local businesses (roofers, car mechanics, HVAC repair, insurance agents) as well as to post reviews and lodge complaints. The BBB warns the public when a company receives a lot of complaints, or when it gets wind of various scams online or in local communities.

IS A BBB SEAL WORTH THE COST?

Given the organization's storied history and high visibility, you might assume that adding a BBB seal to your website would be a no-brainer. The catch is that to display the seal you have to be accredited—and that costs money. Depending on the nature of the accreditation and the size of your business, the cost typically runs between a few hundred and several thousand dollars per year.

So, is it worth it? You can find any number of articles online by those who say it isn't, based on their own experiences. In my research, I've found that the BBB accreditation remains a good value, particularly for the following types of businesses:

- Local service businesses such as contractors, plumbers, restaurants, financial services, doctors, and dentists
- New businesses that have not yet had time to establish a cadence of positive customer reviews on review sites such as Google, Yelp, Tripadvisor, G2, and others
- Ecommerce businesses trying to establish their credibility relative to Amazon and other large players
- Businesses whose clientele is generally age forty plus, the demographic with which BBB carries the most weight

- Businesses for which spending, say, $5,000+ for an annual accreditation fee (this would be a typical fee for a national company with a headquarters in a large metropolitan market) is a minor expenditure within the context of your total marketing budget

Adding a trust badge to your site touting that you are a BBB-accredited company with an A+ rating carries a lot of weight to this day—which is why you should consider it for your business, whether or not you are an online merchant.

The TRUSTe Seal

At the ripe old age of twenty-five, the TRUSTe seal is the grand-daddy of trustmarks. Founded as a nonprofit association, TRUSTe promoted online commerce by helping businesses self-regulate privacy concerns—long before the EU's General Data Protection Regulation (GDPR), the California Consumer Privacy Act (CCPA), and other data privacy regulations.

TRUSTe was a trailblazer from the start. Among its achievements, in 2000 it became the first organization to form a framework encompassing US and European privacy standards. While the company has since rebranded as TrustArc and is now a for-profit business, it maintains the TRUSTe certification program and the mission to help websites earn the trust of their visitors.

As important as privacy was to skeptical consumers in the internet's early days, it's fair to say that issues like how to balance privacy and personalization are even more hotly contested today, with the biggest tech companies in the world on the hot seat. That puts TRUSTe—which offers certifications to demonstrate compliance with GDPR, CCPA, and other regulations and protections—right where the action is.

THE PROLIFERATION OF WEBSITE TRUST SEALS

With the early success of the BBB and TRUSTe seals in increasing ecommerce conversions, many other certifying organizations have emerged over the years with their own seals, badges, and emblems for display on ecommerce and other websites.

In addition to these seals, online merchants often create their own badges to showcase specific promises to their customers, such as money-back guarantees and hassle-free returns.

Today, website trust badges fall into five primary categories:

#1: Security Trust Badges

A "safe checkout" badge indicates that an ecommerce site's checkout process is secure and that customer financial data is protected. The Norton seal is among the most popular trustmarks on the Internet, viewed approximately one hundred million times per day by consumers in 170 countries. The TrustedSite, PayPal, and Shopify seals also communicate trust and security. Brands often display these trust badges near their "Add to Cart" links for maximum impact.

#2: Payment Trust Badges

Consumers are more likely to trust your ecommerce website if you accept widely used forms of payment such as Visa, Mastercard, American Express, PayPal, or Apple Pay. Merchant programs by

Visa and others also protect consumers against fraud, making these trust badges even more reassuring to visitors.

#3: Guarantee Trust Badges

Adding a "30-Day Money-Back Guarantee" or "Free 1-Year Warranty" badge to your site can significantly increase sales by reducing your customer's perceived risk. Standing by your product with a guarantee or warranty also communicates your belief in the product's quality. Merchants typically display this badge prominently on their sites, such as near the checkout button.

#4: Shipping Trust Badges

Offering free shipping and hassle-free returns is another effective way to earn buyer trust. Amazon Prime made free shipping something that many consumers now take for granted. Following suit can greatly reduce shopping-cart abandonment.

#5: Endorsement Trust Badges

People trust what other people say about you more than what you say about yourself. That is the power of third-party validation for brands. Brands can showcase third-party endorsements in myriad ways, from a BBB seal to customer logos, media coverage, and industry awards. Endorsement trust badges are a great visual shortcut to quickly convey your brand's strengths, competencies, and achievements.

THE ETERNAL NEED FOR TRUST SIGNALS

Earlier in this chapter, I noted that wax seals engendered trust in five ways, including:

- ensuring privacy,
- providing security,
- guaranteeing legitimacy,
- offering endorsement, and
- conveying status.

Think about the website trust seals you come across today. How do they work to gain your trust?

The TRUSTe seal ensures your *privacy*.

The Norton and TrustedSite seals provide *security*.

The Better Business Bureau seal guarantees *legitimacy*.

Customer logos offer *endorsement*.

Industry award badges convey *status*.

So you can see that the more things change, the more they stay the same. We look for the same basic types of assurance in building trust today that we did one thousand years ago.

While today you might only come across an actual wax seal on a wedding invitation or other ceremonial document, know that their legacy lives on whenever you go online.

CHAPTER 5

Website Trust Signals— Making Visitors Feel at Home

→ Buyers make judgments about your brand based on their experience on your website.

→ Website trust signals encompass all the elements of design, navigation, and content that influence visitor confidence.

→ Creating a website that builds rapport with visitors while highlighting third-party endorsements is the formula for building trust.

F ew things are more important to a brand's reputation than its website.

And yet too many companies, particularly as they get caught up in the day-to-day of running a business, forget just how central their site is to trust in their organization.

Fairly or unfairly, visitors to your home on the web—and in particular, potential customers—make conscious and unconscious judgments about your company based on their online experience.

WHAT A POOR WEBSITE EXPERIENCE
SAYS ABOUT YOU

If you are not giving your website the attention it deserves in areas like performance, navigation, content, and SEO, your visitors may come away with the following impressions:

Sluggish Load Times = Poor Customer Service

Slow to load sends an unconscious message that you may also be slow to answer the phone, slow to respond to a complaint, or slow to deliver an order.

Confusing Navigation = You Don't Understand Your Customer

It foretells other potential issues for your prospects, such as frustrating calls with salespeople, products that don't do quite what they are expected to do, and policies that aren't quite what they seem.

Infrequent Content Updates = You Are Behind the Innovation Curve

If you can't keep your blog updated, how do I know you keep your product updated? How do I know you keep up with the news and trends in your industry? I don't.

Spelling and Grammatical Mistakes = Shoddy Workmanship

I noticed that you misspelled a word in a home-page headline—so how can I trust you to do a meticulous job on my tax return, kitchen sink, or marketing plan?

Poor Website SEO = You're Not Important

Not paying attention to SEO invites Google to consign your site to the farthest reaches of the web. It's like having your fancy office in a bad neighborhood or having your important business dinner in the booth right next to the men's room.

These aren't glib analogies. They demonstrate how people actually process information—the shortcuts our brains take in forming judgments and making decisions. The "prejudices and symbols and cliches and verbal formulas," as Edward Bernays called them.

They also reflect how visitors learn to trust, or not trust, your brand.

CREATING A TRUST-CENTERED WEBSITE

We learned about the importance of website trust seals in the previous chapter; now let's take a look at the bigger picture. What characteristics of a website engender visitor trust?

Ultimately, a *trust-centered website* must achieve the following three objectives:

1. Impress visitors with quality
2. Establish credibility with third-party validation
3. Build rapport with intimacy

This requires an investment not only in professional design, but in taking the time to understand your audience. Because when your website visitors land on your home page, you want them to feel *at home*.

Trust signals factor into every aspect of design, navigation, content, and coding—even your web address itself. And when you fail to incorporate them strategically and with intention, you leave your website's success to chance.

THE $456,000 TRUST SIGNAL

It's amazing how many brands will spend lavishly on marketing expenses like trade show booths and pay-per-click (PPC) advertising, but when it comes to their website, are regular Scrooges.

For example, I've often had difficulty convincing our midmarket clients of the value of premium, custom photography, especially on the company's *Leadership* or *Team* page.

I usually end up winning the argument, though—after I tell them about my company's own experience.

"Do you know what authentic, high-quality team pictures can add to your bottom line?" I ask.

"No, how much?"

"Well, every case is different, and it's next to impossible to quantify precisely..."

"Exactly! That's why I think..."

I gently interrupt.

"But in the case of Idea Grove, I can answer the question very specifically: $456,000."

That's when I win the argument—and it's a true story.

"I FELT A REAL CONNECTION"

Here's what happened: a few years ago, I got a call from a marketing director at a B2B tech company. She had just completed a three-month agency review process and was down to the final two agencies.

But something didn't feel right. She hadn't forged the personal connection she was seeking with either firm.

So she started Googling and stumbled upon the Idea Grove website.

Like many of our visitors, she went immediately to the second most popular destination on our site: our *Team* page. She liked what she saw and picked up the phone.

"I felt a real connection," she told me. "I got a sense of what you'd be like to work with. And we want our company to communicate that same kind of feeling."

Just a few months prior to this conversation, my agency had invested several thousand dollars in an award-winning portrait photographer for the shoot. He really brought out the team's personalities in their photos—and it paid off.

We soon began a year-long engagement with that marketing director's company, including redesigning her brand's website. Over the course of the relationship, it generated $456,000 in revenue for our agency.

CREATING IMAGES THAT BUILD TRUST

If the right photography on a *Team* page can do so much to earn trust (and win business), think of how important the right visuals can be for the rest of your site—your home page, for example.

Have you ever visited the website for a physician's practice or health-tech company and come face to face with a home-page hero image that looks like this?

What exactly have we learned from this image—arguably the *single most viewed element* of your entire website?

Nada.

Zip.

Zilch.

Diddly-squat.

Why on earth would you waste the most important real estate on your website on a generic stock image that literally any other healthcare company could also download from Shutterstock and use on its site as well?

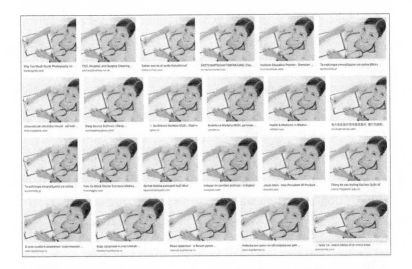

It's the worst possible way to set yourself apart—and also the worst way to establish trust.

When people come to your website, they want to learn about you—in words *and* pictures:

- They want to see photos of your team.
- They want to see videos of your product or service in action.
- They want to see your offices and facilities.
- They want to see detailed testimonials accompanied by the smiling faces of actual happy customers.

All of this imagery helps to tell your unique story. It also communicates that your visitors are not just coming to a nameless, faceless website. They are visiting your online home, where they can learn who you are and what you're about.

Authentic imagery also improves ecommerce sales. A 2019 Cornell Tech study found that on secondhand marketplaces like eBay, sellers who post their own high-quality images of products are trusted far more than those who post either stock photos of those same products or poor-quality photos (Lefkowitz). Because online visitors can't see and touch your product in the real world, custom imagery fills a critical gap in building trust.

That's not to say that stock photos don't serve a purpose. It makes sense to use them when it would simply be too difficult or expensive to use custom photography. A frequently updated blog, for example, will typically need to rely on stock photography. Even some of the most popular news sites in the world use stock photography to illustrate their content for this very reason.

But the most important images on your site—those on your home page, your *About Us* page, your *Team* page, and your product pages—should focus on *you*, not the latest pics on iStock.

TOP TWENTY-FOUR WEBSITE
TRUST SIGNALS

Custom photography is only one of the website trust signals you should use to build a trust-centered website. Here are twenty-four trust signals that can make a big difference for your site's performance:

#1: Trusted Top-Level Domain (TLD)

Research shows that fully three-quarters of website visitors trust brands with *.com* domains more than those with lesser-known TLDs. While alternatives can work well in certain sectors—such as *.io* and *.ai* with technology companies—it's often worth spending what it takes to secure a trusted *.com* domain. TLDs frequently used by spam sites, like *.info*, should be avoided.

#2: Fast Page Loading

One way to make a good first impression is to build a site that loads quickly. The likelihood of users leaving your site increases by 32 percent when your page load time increases from one to three seconds, according to Google. If it takes much longer than that, you might as well close up shop.

#3: Professional Design

Invest in a quality, custom design. If your website looks like it was slapped together with little care and attention to detail, that's exactly what a visitor will think of you and your product.

#4: Clean Navigation

Deliver a simple, intuitive user experience with easy conversion paths. This suggests transparency to your visitors and makes them more comfortable filling out a form or completing a purchase.

NAVIGATING YOUR WAY TO TRUST—
AND CONVERSIONS

Sometimes when I visit a corporate website, I am so disoriented by the stiff language and confusing navigation paths that I am reminded of Jane Austen's famous line from *Northanger Abbey*, when Catherine apologizes to the older, more sophisticated Henry for her inability to comprehend his meaning.

"I do not understand you," she says.

"Then we are on very unequal terms, for I understand you perfectly well," Henry replies.

"Me?—yes; I cannot speak well enough to be unintelligible."

Boom.

Working in B2B technology, I've dealt with my fair share of clients who have difficulty communicating what they do, and why they do it, in intelligible terms. This can lead to website copy that is needlessly indirect and obtuse.

The problem doesn't always stop there, either. It can afflict a website's navigation as well.

Three Hurdles to Trust

When marketers talk about website conversion paths, the conversation typically focuses on lead generation. But that's actually only the second most important reason your website should have simple and clean navigation. The first is trust.

Visitors don't want to be confused, tricked, or surprised as they navigate your site. Here's how to avoid each of those frustrating hurdles on the path to visitor trust:

#1: Don't Confuse Your Visitors

Research by the Nielsen Norman Group concludes that users almost always approach a new website with a skeptical mindset (Kaley and Nielsen 2019). They expect to be disappointed. The best way to earn their trust (and increase their time on your site), is to provide an intuitive experience. The word "intuitive" is so overused in design that it's become almost meaningless, but what we're really talking about is providing an experience that *isn't confusing*. This tells the visitor you're on their wavelength.

#2: Don't Trick Your Visitors

As all marketers should know by now, popups and banners flying across your website can trigger an immediate loss of trust and increase in bounce rates. Visitors have heard enough horror stories about data breaches that they don't want to feel tricked into providing personal data. A classic example of this is the clumsy way that many ecommerce sites make "free" offers that ultimately require the entry of credit-card information or other commitments. Better to be up front if you want to build visitor trust.

#3: Don't Surprise Your Visitors

Visitors should have the opportunity to convert at all the places they would expect to, so while it's natural to want your design to stand out, you still want it to feel familiar. Some of the most common ways that sites give unwelcome surprises to their visitors are non-standardized layouts and conflicting calls to action. Content that is off-topic or off in tone can also drive visitors away.

When it comes to navigation, remember Catherine's response to Henry and keep it simple—if you want your visitors' trust.

#5: High-Quality Content

Your content should make visitors feel like they've come to the right place. Website content that is overly salesy, or blog content that is overly vague, will drive them away. Spelling and grammatical mistakes are a trust killer as well. Visitors notice when a site's content appears out of date, too, so keep it fresh.

#6: *About Us* Page

Share your company's origin story in a personal way, as you might tell it to a friend at a party. Add names, events, and little details that make your history feel authentic and unique.

#7: *Leadership* or *Team* Page

These pages are among the most visited, particularly for B2B brands, because customers want to see who they will be buying from or working with. Add certification badges to leadership or team bios to communicate instant credibility to visitors.

#8: *Contact Us* Page

Make it easy for visitors to reach you, by offering multiple modes of contact: phone, email, live chat, and a form they can fill out to be contacted later. Add your location, along with photos or a map, for those who want to visit you in person or at least know where you can be found.

#9: Personalized Experience

Where possible, deliver personalized experiences to visitors based on browsing behavior and other clues—without being too creepy about it.

#10: Custom Photography

As discussed earlier in this chapter, it's OK to include stock photography on your website, but balance this with your own photographs to create trust. Include pictures of your offices, products, employees, and customers to help your visitors get to know you better.

#11: Customer Logos

For B2B companies, one of the most valuable trust signals is client or customer logos. Prominently display the names and logos of well-known brands on your site to attract more of the same.

#12: Celebrity/Influencer Endorsements

If respected public figures endorse your product, feature their photos and endorsements prominently, and consider testimonial videos in which they describe their experience with your product or service in detail.

#13: Customer Case Studies

Case studies serve three important functions:

1. They show a use case of what you do.
2. They demonstrate concrete results and goals met.
3. They include a customer recommendation.

Publish at least one case study for every major use case and make it easy for your visitors to find. The more case studies, the better.

#14: Customer Testimonials

These are endorsement quotes from satisfied customers. They don't go into the same level of detail as a case study, but for a visitor scanning your website, they quickly establish credibility. As with case studies, the more testimonials, the better.

#15: Embedded Customer Reviews

Many review sites, such as Tripadvisor, G2, and TrustRadius, enable you to embed customer reviews on your website. You earn trust with your visitors in two ways: (1) by providing third-party validation and (2) by pulling this validation directly from a respected, neutral source.

#16: First-Party Customer Reviews

Third-party sites aren't the only way to collect customer reviews. You can also solicit reviews directly on your site; these are known as first-party reviews. They've been common on high-volume ecommerce sites for years—but now businesses ranging from restaurants to SaaS companies are getting in on the action.

#17: Icons Linking to Active Social Media Channels

Few things cause visitors to question your trustworthiness more than abandoned or nonexistent social channels. Be sure to post regularly on the channels that matter most to your customers and include links to these accounts from your website's header, footer, or blog.

#18: Social Proof Statistics and Notifications

Statistics that show your sales, downloads, subscribers, or followers create a bandwagon effect that makes visitors more likely to buy from you.

WOO BUYERS ONTO YOUR BANDWAGON WITH THESE WEBSITE TRUST SIGNALS

"He's such a bandwagon."

That's what my thirteen-year-old son says when one of his friends claims to be a University of Virginia basketball fan—*after* the team's first NCAA championship in 2019. My son has been following the team since he was in diapers and has endured his share of ups and downs.

While long-suffering sports fans of a suddenly hot team may resent the Johnny-come-latelies, the bandwagon effect can be a big boost for brands. It's a powerful psychological phenomenon whereby consumers do something mostly because other people are doing it—even to the point of ignoring or overriding their previous beliefs.

The term dates back to the nineteenth century. Bandwagons were parade floats on which revelers played music and celebrated—and encouraged observers to jump aboard. Today, the bandwagon appeal has become a bedrock strategy of the advertising and marketing world.

While we all like to think we make our own decisions, the truth is we find comfort and assurance in following others. People conform in order to be liked or accepted. It's also a reasonable shortcut to take during the buying process; if so many customers like a particular product, most buyers figure it's probably a solid, low-risk choice for them, too.

In a sense, all forms of third-party validation exploit the band-wagon effect. People want to hear what other people think of you before doing business with you. "Other people" include the news media, influencers, analysts, experts—and especially your customers. That's why testimonials, case studies, and media coverage are so effective in creating website trust.

Volume, Volume, Volume

The ultimate power of the bandwagon appeal, however, is in volume—the quantity of endorsers rather than the quality of their endorsements. It's less about an individual customer story or positive review, and more about the sheer number of people who buy your product or interact with your brand.

If you are in a volume business, expressing your success quantitatively is the best way to woo new customers onto your bandwagon. And if you can communicate your brand's popularity in a dynamic way—such as with real-time statistics—it's all the better.

Here are four ways to leverage the bandwagon effect, which you may wish to feature on your home page or, if you have an ecommerce site, during the checkout process:

#1: Social Media Follower Statistics

Show the number of followers or subscribers your company has on LinkedIn, Twitter, Facebook, Instagram, YouTube, and/or TikTok to indicate that you are a popular brand.

#2: Product Sales Statistics

Share and frequently update how many customers you have and/or the number of products purchased ("over 100 billion burgers sold").

#3: Subscriber and Download Statistics

Let visitors know how many people have subscribed to your blog or newsletter or downloaded your latest tip sheet, guide, or industry report.

#4: Real-Time Social Proof Notifications

Particularly for ecommerce sites with brisk sales, displaying customer actions like downloads and purchases as they happen can have a real bandwagon effect on site visitors. They feel the momentum and want to be part of it.

Bottom line: if you are generating sizable numbers in sales and/or customer engagement, don't be shy about sharing them.

#19: "As Seen In" Media Logos

One of the longest-standing forms of third-party validation is news coverage. Visitors are more likely to believe your company is doing something right if it has attracted positive attention from industry publications, local TV stations, or other media outlets. Display their logos prominently.

#20: Industry Association Logos

Being part of well-known industry associations can carry a lot of weight, particularly for smaller companies and consultants. Display these logos to borrow the authority of the groups your customers know and respect.

#21: Partnership and Co-Branded Logos

Earn trust with badges and logos that highlight your status as an official partner of well-known brands. In B2B technology, for example, the partner networks of Microsoft, Oracle, and Cisco confer authority on member companies.

#22: Industry Award Logos

Award logos send a message of credibility and accomplishment to website visitors, particularly if those awards are difficult to win, relevant to your brand, and respected in your industry. Display award badges prominently on your home page, *About Us* page, or payment page.

#23: Trust Seals

As covered in the last chapter, certification or accreditation badges from Norton, the Better Business Bureau, TrustedSite, Visa, PayPal, etc., demonstrate that your site is safe and your brand is legit.

#24: The Ps and Qs

While they are often afterthoughts for marketers, having an up-to-date privacy policy, terms and conditions for your website's use, and a copyright with the current year displayed are all important trust signals. Paying attention to these details communicates thoroughness and respect for your visitors.

MASTERING THE TRUST PLAYING FIELD

Buyers make conscious and unconscious judgments about your business based on their experience on your website. Creating a website that impresses visitors with quality, establishes credibility with third-party endorsement, and builds rapport with intimacy is the ideal formula for earning trust.

If the long list of website trust signals outlined in this chapter leaves you wondering where to start, don't worry. I don't expect you to be able to deploy all of these trust signals on your website.

For example:

- If you're a startup, you might not have customers to provide logos, testimonials, or case studies yet.
- If your company sells million-dollar software with long sales cycles, you're unlikely to have the volume of activity necessary to show real-time social proof.
- If your customer reviews are poor, you probably don't want to highlight them on your website until you address your reputation issues.

And that's OK.

Before you can master the game, you first have to understand the playing field. By the end of this book, you'll have a rock-solid framework for building, growing, and protecting your brand with trust. We'll discuss this system as it relates to web design in Chapter 13, "Making Connections: User Experience."

CHAPTER 6

Inbound Trust Signals— Laying the Breadcrumb Path

→ Inbound trust signals form the breadcrumb path that leads visitors to your website—and buyers to purchase.

→ Buyers are guided by the sources of information within their continuums of influence.

→ Inbound trust signals include third-party endorsements from the media, influencers, customers—and even Google.

In the Brothers Grimm fairy tale *Hansel and Gretel,* Medieval Germany is in the grips of famine, and a woodcutter's family is starving. The woodcutter and his wife plot to abandon their children, Hansel and Gretel, deep in the forest so they will have fewer mouths to feed. But Hansel overhears the plot and leaves a trail of breadcrumbs in the woods so he and Gretel can find their way home.

Unfortunately, the crumbs are eaten by birds and the children get lost. They must defeat a wicked witch to ultimately escape being cooked and eaten themselves.

Although Hansel's plan was foiled, today the idea of following a "breadcrumb trail" to a destination or decision is one just about everyone is familiar with.

In digital marketing, breadcrumb paths are most closely associated with web navigation. But there is another way to think of breadcrumbs in marketing.

In *Hansel and Gretel*, the children leave a path of food, in the form of breadcrumbs, to guide them home at a time of great famine.

Today, successful brands leave a trail of breadcrumbs, in the form of *inbound trust signals,* to guide their buyers to purchase—at a time when trust appears to be in short supply.

FROM INBOUND MARKETING TO INBOUND TRUST SIGNALS

When HubSpot co-founders Brian Halligan and Dharmesh Shah coined the term "inbound marketing" in 2005, their notion was that consumers were tired of being interrupted by marketers and pestered by salespeople—and that the better way to reach them was through helpful, non-salesy content and conversation.

By helping these consumers, brands could lure them "inbound" to their website.

I view inbound marketing through a specific lens—one that puts trust front and center. That's why I believe that the best marketing programs focus on laying a path of inbound trust signals—the trust breadcrumbs that attract interested visitors to your website.

FOLLOWING THE BREADCRUMBS TO A NEW CRIB MATTRESS

Earlier this year, one of Idea Grove's account managers, Laurie Lane, had a baby girl. In the months leading up to the new arrival, she and her husband set a budget and began building out a nursery in their home. Among the items on their shopping list: a crib mattress.

To stay within budget, the couple initially decided to seek out the least expensive mattress they could find. But then Laurie remembered an Instagram post from one of her favorite creators recommending a specific mattress as being the safest on the market.

Laurie couldn't recall the name of the mattress, so she Googled "safest crib mattresses." Her memory was refreshed when the brand turned up high in search results. She then found hundreds of four- and five-star reviews from this brand's customers across numerous sites.

Next, she saw positive coverage of the mattress in *Parents* magazine. Finally, she noticed that a celebrity she respected, an Olympic gymnast, had partnered with the brand and offered a testimonial based on her own experience.

Laurie and her husband ended up spending twice as much as they'd planned for their baby's mattress—but they were confident they had made the right choice.

In Chapter 2, I introduced the concept of a *continuum of influence*. For Laurie, the continuum in this case included:

- an Instagram creator, who introduced her to the brand;
- Google, which elevated the brand in search results;
- customers, who gave five-star reviews to the mattress online;
- a news source, which gave the brand positive coverage; and
- a celebrity athlete, who partnered with the brand.

Each of these sources laid a breadcrumb along Laurie's ultimate path to purchase.

Traditional PR people, ask yourself this: if Laurie had only seen the coverage in *Parents* magazine but nothing else, would it have been enough to push her to purchase?

Probably not. That's why it's so important for PR practitioners to embrace the buyer's full continuum of influence in our efforts—if we want them to have the intended result.

THE YELPIFICATION OF THE INTERNET

In a world where gatekeepers like media critics, analysts, and experts have been knocked off their high horses, the public turns first to their peers for advice on products and brands. And today, the most powerful form of peer influence is customer reviews.

Most consumers today trust online reviews from strangers as much as the advice of friends and family. Compared to traditional word-of-mouth referrals, online reviews are easier to access and more likely to include use cases that are relevant to the buyer.

The first major success story in the review-site space was Yelp, founded in 2004 to provide crowdsourced recommendations for local businesses and services. It went public in 2012 with a $1.5 billion valuation. At the time, it had twenty-two million reviews on its site, attracting sixty-one million unique monthly visitors.

Today, despite intense competition from Google, Facebook, Amazon, Tripadvisor, and others, Yelp draws 180 million unique monthly visitors to more than 225 million reviews on its site.

Meanwhile, the public's trust in online reviews now extends beyond local restaurants, hotels, and service businesses to virtually every industry and product—from vegan ice cream brands, which you can compare at Influenster, to multimillion-dollar enterprise software, which you can review at Gartner Peer Insights, PeerSpot, and other sites.

My own agency focuses on B2B technology, where, driven by the explosion of SaaS products, review sites like G2, Capterra, and TrustRadius now far surpass the influence of traditional gatekeepers, such as industry analysts and computer magazines.

Chicago-based G2, in fact, appears to be replicating the Yelp story in the B2B tech space, having now raised more than $250 million on a valuation of more than $1.1 billion. The site hosts more than 1.5 million reviews.

THE STRANGE CASE OF FEATUREDCUSTOMERS

The success of review sites, from Yelp to G2, is powerful testament to the fact that people trust what other people say about you more than what you say about yourself.

That's why even when Google users search for your brand by name, they will likely read content about your company on other sites before visiting yours. And if they don't like what they find, they probably won't visit you at all.

Did you know there is a successful website, FeaturedCustomers, that appears, at first glance, to be another B2B tech review site, but that actually gathers no original reviews itself? It has built its entire business by scraping and resharing testimonials and customer stories from the websites of B2B tech companies. It has aggregated more than 1.3 million customer references, testimonials, and success stories in this way.

How does FeaturedCustomers make money?

By charging B2B tech brands for sponsorships—*of their own republished content*!

This business model works brilliantly because it understands buyer psychology—specifically, that the *exact* same stories about your brand are more trusted when they appear on someone else's website.

TOP TWENTY INBOUND TRUST SIGNALS

If web users are more likely to trust the same testimonial for your brand, from the same customer, simply because it is hosted on somebody else's site, that tells you how essential inbound trust signals are to building, growing, and protecting your brand.

Inbound trust signals are all forms of third-party validation, and the most important of these are media coverage, influencer endorsements, customer reviews, and Google visibility.

Let's take a closer look at twenty specific trust signals to drive interest in your brand and traffic to your website:

#1: Media Coverage

Few forms of third-party validation are as powerful as coverage in well-known media, such as daily newspapers, national business publications, and respected trade journals. This is why so many brands invest in PR agencies for media relations.

#2: Press Releases

Press releases can be helpful in establishing credibility, especially if they are distributed by major wire services such as PR Newswire and Business Wire, which have higher standards for acceptance. Wire releases are also more likely to appear in Google News results.

#3: Bylined Articles and Op-eds

When you submit an article that appears in a business or industry publication, you earn credibility as a thought leader with potential buyers.

#4: Blog Guest Posts

Many bloggers in your field may be open to you providing a guest post, which can achieve similar benefits to a bylined article. But tread carefully: if Google decides you are littering the web with keyword-stuffed guest posts just to rank higher in search results, you may be penalized for it.

#5: Sponsored Content

Today, publications like *Forbes*, *Entrepreneur*, and *Fast Company* have paid programs that give you special access to submit or be quoted in stories. These typically appear in Google News results.

WHY FORBES COUNCILS IS A NO-BRAINER
FOR THOUGHT LEADERSHIP

As the blurring of earned media and paid media accelerates, the once bright line between editorial content and advertising is rapidly fading. Unfortunately for journalistic purists, most news consumers appear to be unconcerned about this trend—they believe they are perfectly capable of distinguishing between what information is credible and what isn't.

Once again, the gatekeepers lose and the crowd wins.

While many public relations practitioners—like most journalists—bemoan this trend, the PR agency's first obligation is to serve its clients, using the tools that best help clients reach their goals today.

That's why augmenting your earned media efforts with a membership in Forbes Councils or similar programs is a no-brainer for thought leadership marketing campaigns today.

Sponsored Content Loses Stigma, Gains Trust

What's known as *native advertising* or *sponsored content* today used to be called *advertorial.* In the old days, advertorial content was often pretty horrible. It was thinly veiled advertising and lacked the same quality standards as editorial content—so much so that it stood out like a sore thumb. It was also clearly labeled as advertorial, further separating it from earned media content.

Particularly since the emergence of BuzzFeed in 2013, native advertising has become far more sophisticated and helpful to readers, which in turn has reduced its stigma. And while most outlets still label their sponsored content as such, it now blends in much more effortlessly with the editorial copy around it.

Put another way, as native advertising has shed its stigma, it has gained audience trust.

Forbes Councils, managed by the Community Company on behalf of *Forbes*, further elevates sponsored content by making it more than a simple pay-for-play transaction. Forbes Councils calls itself an "exclusive membership organization" in which the opportunity to publish content on Forbes.com is one of the benefits.

The Value of Visibility through Forbes Councils

In addition to being an ingenious business model, Forbes Councils is also far more accessible to midsize and smaller businesses than many brand-name sponsored-content programs. Many of the top outlets won't work with a company without an investment of $50,000 or more; the cost of a Forbes Councils membership, by contrast, is less than $3,000 per year.

And it's hard to argue the value of the visibility and credibility that *Forbes* provides. The modest annual investment earns you the opportunity to publish as many as ten to twelve articles per year with your byline on the *Forbes* website. These articles appear in Google News results and in LinkedIn's Mentioned in the News, earning the authority and trust that come with those placements.

There is also the opportunity to appear as often as several times per month in "expert panels"—roundup stories on topics relevant to your field.

Keep in mind that with both the bylined articles and the expert panels, *Forbes* doesn't guarantee that it will publish your content if it doesn't meet its standards. Indeed, Forbes Councils' editors may kick back your articles for multiple rounds of revisions to make sure they are non-promotional, meet quality standards, and are deemed to be genuinely helpful to readers.

The Forbes Councils model has been so successful that the Community Company has launched a similar program with local business journals in cities nationwide, called the Business Journals Leadership Trust, as well as programs with *Fast Company, Newsweek,* and *Rolling Stone. Entrepreneur* and other publications offer similar programs.

#6: Celebrity and Influencer Endorsements

Especially in fashion, beauty, food, and travel, but now across virtually all industries, influencer endorsements on social media—whether paid or unpaid—carry real weight with buyers.

#7: Social Media Accounts

An active presence on major social media platforms, including LinkedIn, Twitter, Facebook, Instagram, and YouTube, is advisable for most brands. Your customers and prospects expect to see you in these places, and if you're not there they'll wonder why.

#8: Social Media Responsiveness

Many buyers check out your social channels to see whether

customers are tagging you with complaints, and if they are, how well and how quickly you respond to them.

#9: Google Business Profile

When people search for your brand by name, think of that first page of results as your "second home page." For businesses with local offices, your Google Business Profile should be that page's centerpiece.

#10: Google Maps Listing

When you search for a local business, the top three results will appear with a map at the top of the first page. Securing your place in this "Google 3-Pack" is great for trust—and even better for traffic.

#11: Google Reviews

Google has surpassed both Yelp and Facebook in reviews, with those results appearing in your Google Business Profile and Google Maps listings. They're a must for most brands today.

#12: Customer Reviews on Relevant Sites

Review sites have become part of the decision-making process for virtually every product and industry. See which sites come up in your first three pages of branded search results—then reach out to your customers to contribute reviews.

#13: Glassdoor Reviews

When people search for a company by name, Glassdoor is often one of the top results. Earning five-star reviews from your current and former employees is not just valuable for recruiting; it's important to winning new customers as well. Buyers are more likely to trust you if you treat your people right.

#14: Participation in Online Forums

From LinkedIn and Facebook groups to industry-specific forums, your company's team can build relationships and gain credibility for your brand by joining the discussion.

#15: Participation in Industry Events

When you participate in trade shows, virtual conferences, and other industry events as a speaker, sponsor, or exhibitor, you often receive an endorsement on the event's website or in press releases, generating trust online and off.

#16: Directory Listings

Local and industry-specific business directories are an easy, typically free or inexpensive way to increase authority and visibility. But be warned: some business directories are scams. Check the site's domain authority on Moz as a quick way to see if a listing has value.

#17: Wikipedia Entry

Securing an entry for your business in Wikipedia, the most popular reference site in the world, establishes your brand's authority. The site's editors carefully screen submissions to ensure they meet "notability" criteria. Earning media coverage and other forms of third-party validation is a prerequisite to inclusion.

LANDING A WIKIPEDIA PAGE:
IT'S COMPLICATED

Beyond media coverage, online reviews, influencer endorsements, and Google visibility, a wide range of other sources of trust serve as inbound trust signals. Some of these are easier to attain than others.

One of the most coveted by many of my agency's clients over the years has been a Wikipedia page.

"Can you get my company in Wikipedia," they ask?

My answer is always the same: *"It's complicated."*

My Long, Strange Trip with Wikipedia

In February 2005, immediately upon founding my PR agency as a solo consultancy, I successfully listed Idea Grove on Wikipedia. The glowing reference included links to my brand-new, bare-bones website.

Those were simpler times, of course.

Soon enough, an overwhelming deluge of companies and SEO practitioners got in the Wikipedia game, forcing Wikipedia to tighten its policies. The site began to enforce stricter standards of "notability" as a requirement to be included in the encyclopedia.

It also classified its outbound links as "no follow" links with search engines to prevent SEO firms from gaming the resource. And it implemented a sweeping conflict-of-interest policy that discouraged individuals, companies, and their representatives from editing their own entries.

This basically shut marketers and PR professionals out of Wikipedia—at least theoretically.

How to Handle—or Not Handle—Wikipedia

Although Wikipedia links no longer carry the SEO benefits they once did, Wikipedia's higher standards for entries have made the encyclopedia an important gatekeeper for determining what companies and people are notable or prominent.

As just one example of Wikipedia's clout, Twitter recently stated that having a Wikipedia page helps qualify organizations and individuals for its verified badge—the famous blue checkmark.

So, how does a marketer go about getting their company in Wikipedia? As I said, it's complicated.

I love Wikipedia; I truly do. It's a wonderful resource and amazing achievement. Heck, it's the third-most-trafficked site in the world.

But it's like sausage—sometimes you love it a little less once you know how it's made.

Wikipedia is a sprawling community of more than 130,000 volunteer editors with competing agendas, axes to grind, varying perspectives on who and what deserves a Wikipedia listing, and an even wider range of ideas about how those entries should be written.

More often than not, though, the wisdom of the crowd prevails over time. That's why Wikipedia, founded in 2001, is both the father of crowdsourcing and crowdsourcing's greatest success story.

For most of its history, Wikipedia has taken a strong position against PR agencies, SEO firms, corporate marketing departments, or anyone else who has a financial interest in a Wikipedia entry creating or editing that entry. The current policy states as follows:

> Conflict of interest (COI) editing involves contributing to Wikipedia about yourself, family, friends, clients, employers, or your financial and other relationships. Any external relationship can trigger a conflict of interest…COI editing is strongly discouraged on Wikipedia…
>
> For example, an article about a band should not be written by the band's manager, and a biography should not be an autobiography or written by the subject's spouse. There can be a COI when writing on behalf of a competitor or opponent of the page subject, just as there is when writing on behalf of the page subject…
> COI emerges from an editor's roles and relationships, and the tendency to bias that we assume exists when those roles and relationships conflict. (Wikipedia 2022)

Wikipedia does make exceptions for what it calls "uncontroversial" edits by COI editors, but these exceptions are extremely limited in scope:

> Editors who have a general conflict of interest may make unambiguously uncontroversial edits. They may…remove spam and unambiguous vandalism, fix spelling and grammatical errors, repair broken links, and add independent reliable sources when another editor has requested them…

The bottom line is: creating or editing your company's own Wikipedia entry is highly discouraged and can lead to your entry being removed or your account being blocked.

Wikipedia Risks and Rewards

Having said that, the surreptitious creation and editing of Wikipedia entries on behalf of clients is a staple of the online reputation management (ORM) business, and if you run a simple Google search for ORM firms, you'll find many who freely promote their Wikipedia services.

Should you partake of these services and create Wikipedia entries on the sly? You could—but it's important to know the risks.

An agency called Wiki-PR boasted, a few years ago, that it could create Wikipedia entries for companies through its "network of established editors." It claimed clients like Viacom and Priceline, along with many smaller companies. Wikipedia ended up identifying and banning Wiki-PR's editors and pulling down hundreds of Wikipedia entries. It was an embarrassment for those involved—although the practice has not stopped and probably won't.

If you want to participate in Wikipedia, I would suggest that the best way to do so is to do it transparently. Create an account, identify yourself, disclose any conflicts of interest in your account profile, and then edit away. If you are careful, incremental, and make every effort to be objective, your participation may be accepted.

#18: Community Involvement

Pursuing a social-purpose strategy that includes sponsoring or volunteering for nonprofit organizations can earn visibility on the nonprofit's website and social media channels—as well as build goodwill in your community.

#19: Top Ranking for Branded Search Queries

A high percentage of Google queries are searches for brands or specific websites ("youtube" and "facebook" are the top two Google searches). When someone enters the name of your company or product in search, make sure your site comes up first in the results.

#20: High Ranking for Industry Keywords

Ranking among the top results for common search terms in your market segment not only greatly increases your website traffic but also confers authority on your brand.

THE BREADCRUMBS THAT MATTER MOST

If Hansel and Gretel got lost in the woods today, they would probably just pull out their smartphones and enter their home address in Google Maps.

But if they were looking for the best place to find candy (with no witches in the vicinity), they would likely seek out online reviews, media reports, and other inbound trust signals. Those are the breadcrumbs that matter most to consumers in 2022.

CHAPTER 7

SEO Trust Signals— For Google's Eyes Only

→ Trust signals are not just important to humans; they are vital to Google's search algorithm, too.

→ SEO trust signals are hidden signals that Google uses to enhance the quality of search results.

→ These signals include domain age, mobile friendliness, and branded search volume, among others.

In scholarly circles, academics have long relied on citations of their work by others in their field as trust signals. Having your research cited is the currency of academia. It can lead to prestigious awards, better jobs, and higher salaries.

This is what gave Stanford PhD students Larry Page and Sergey Brin the idea for Google in 1996.

The search engine's founders reasoned that the best way to rank websites was to measure the number and quality of citations—in the form of hyperlinks—to these sites. They assumed the most important sites were likely to receive more inbound links, in the same way the most important academic papers were referenced more often by peers.

If something sounds familiar about this approach, it's because it's been a core theme of this book. Google was founded as a *third-party endorsement algorithm*. It used, and continues to use, third-party validation to determine the sites it trusts and how much it trusts them to deliver the best results for any given search.

A THIRD-PARTY ENDORSEMENT ALGORITHM

In the same way that you are more likely to trust a brand that has received positive reviews, social media buzz, or media coverage, Google sees links from other sites as endorsements.

And just as an endorsement from a top publication or influencer carries more weight than that of a single review, links from top sites have a bigger impact on search than links from sites with little influence or traffic.

In the early days, Google could only comprehend the basics of language and could only differentiate one website from another based on the number of links coming and going from each site. The gaps in Google's algorithm were exploited by the fledgling SEO industry, which developed sketchy tactics such as link farms, link spam, and keyword stuffing to trick Google into ranking content higher than it deserved to be.

Google realized that this kind of deception was a threat to its very existence. Brin said in an interview that the company couldn't survive "if people didn't trust us" (Eadicicco 2014).

FIGHTING SPAMMERS WITH ALGORITHM UPDATES

Google fought back against the bad actors with what became known as the "Google Florida Update" of its algorithm in 2003, which punished spammy sites in search results. It has been issuing regular algorithm updates to improve the quality of users' search experience ever since.

Today, Google's algorithm is very close to reading text as well as a human being. It is as annoyed as you are by keyword stuffing —the practice where the same keywords are used over and over again on a page to catch Google's attention. Just as you respond to keyword stuffing by leaving the page, Google responds by making the page less visible in search results.

Since Google's improvements have made its algorithm more humanlike in how it rates and responds to content, it should come as no surprise that most of Google's trust signals are the same as those that humans use to determine which websites to trust. They're the kinds of trust signals we've been discussing throughout this book.

Google looks for websites that provide a good user experience —for example, sites with loads of well-organized content that is relevant for your users. And it looks for references (ideally with links) to your site in established sources, such as respected media outlets, industry blogs, and directories. It even takes your Google reviews and star ratings, as well as reviews on other sites, into account in its rankings.

GOOGLE'S HIDDEN TRUST SIGNALS

While many of the specific signals Google looks for in determining its level of trust in your brand are also seen by your visitors, others are more hidden. Google sees them, but users likely don't.

These SEO trust signals fall into three primary categories: domain characteristics, website characteristics, and engagement characteristics.

Domain Characteristics

While users may look at domain signals such as the credibility of your top-level domain (*.com* versus *.info*, for example), Google can also look at signs that aren't so visible, such as your domain's age and length of registration.

Website Characteristics

Google looks at your site's architecture, mobile friendliness, and, of course, backlink profile. Google also considers your site's reputation history—whether your brand has ever been penalized for SEO misdeeds in the past.

Engagement Characteristics

While links remain a critical measure of the popularity of your site, Google now incorporates actual traffic data for a fuller view. The more engagement and interest in your site, the better.

I should add that Google is often pretty cagey about acknowledging the importance of these hidden signals—or even whether they use them at all. Google's algorithm has been gamed by the SEO industry for so long, the search giant is cautious about sharing information that can be exploited to diminish the quality of results.

TOP TWELVE SEO TRUST SIGNALS

Based on the empirical research of SEO experts, here are a dozen of the most important hidden trust signals:

#1: Backlink Quality

Backlinks (also called *inbound links*) are links from other websites to yours. Just as customers are influenced by news media coverage of your brand, Google trusts you more when authoritative sources link to your site.

#2: Backlink Quantity and Diversity

The more quality backlinks you earn, the better. Google also prefers the links to come from a diverse range of sites. This suggests you accumulated the links organically rather than through nefarious means, such as buying them.

#3: Domain Age

Google figures you are not a fly-by-night operation if your domain has been around a long time.

GOOGLE LIKES DOMAINS THAT
WEREN'T BORN YESTERDAY

A controversial Google ranking factor that is little-known to most marketers, but hotly debated among SEO geeks, is *domain age*—the length of time your website's domain has been registered.

Some claim domain age is extremely important to how much Google trusts your site and to how well it ranks. Others cite Google executive John Mueller (2019), who has stated that "domain age helps nothing" in search results.

Somewhere in the middle is former Google search-quality guru Matt Cutts (2010), who has said that newly registered domains generally have to establish themselves for at least a couple months before being on equal footing with older domains.

Cutts' recommendation is that as soon as you buy a domain, it's best to launch a "coming soon" landing page so that by the time you have your website built and ready to publish, your site will be in a better position to rank.

Of course, Google's algorithm is notorious for being a black box—and Google likes it that way. Google's engineers don't want it to be gamed or reverse engineered, so it's not unusual to receive less-than-crystal-clear responses to seemingly straightforward questions like, "Does domain age matter?"

Based on my own research and applying a little common sense, here's my advice as it relates to domain age:

- Your domain's age is a factor for Google and for your brand equity; the longer your domain is established, the better.

- If you are a new business, it may be useful to buy an *aged domain* for your business rather than registering a new one, but research shows it's really only helpful if relevant links are already pointing to the domain.
- If you are interested in a rebrand and new domain, simply redirecting your previous brand domain to the new domain should be sufficient to recoup any credit Google gives for domain age.

Early in 2021, Google seemed to finally confirm the importance of domain age when it introduced "About this result," a popup feature next to individual search results that is designed to provide users more context about a site or company they haven't heard of before.

In an environment where visitors have become less trusting of the content they find online, Google's stated purpose for adding "About this result" was to empower users to vet the sites they are considering visiting before they click.

The "About this result" box typically contains four pieces of information:

1. The domain or website's age, as measured by Google's date of first indexation
2. Whether or not the site is secure, as measured by the presence of an SSL certificate
3. Google's basic reasoning for displaying the result ("the website matches one or more of your search terms")
4. A note that the result is organic and not a paid ad

For brands or websites that have their own Wikipedia pages, the first couple of sentences of the Wikipedia entry will typically replace the information on domain age. Google's point of view, it would seem, is that in the absence of a Wikipedia entry, the date of first indexation is a pretty good substitute for establishing trust.

#4: Length of Registration

When you register your domain not for one year, but for five or ten, that tells Google you plan on sticking around.

#5: Reputation History

If your site has been penalized for violating Google's webmaster guidelines, consider yourself on probation when it comes to earning the search giant's trust. Stay on your best behavior.

#6: Mobile Friendliness

Google now uses the mobile version of your site for most indexing and ranking, so making sure your site works well for smartphone users is critical.

#7: HTML and Architecture Signals

Google trusts sites with concise, relevant titles, descriptions, and headings. Google also looks at site speed, accessibility, clean URL structure, 404 errors, and the presence of an HTML or XML sitemap.

#8: Branded Searches

In determining your site's authority, Google factors in the number of times people search for your brand by name. The more branded searches, the more trusted the brand.

#9: Brand-Plus-Keyword Searches

Google looks at searches that combine your brand name with keywords to assess the topics and industries in which you have the most authority.

GOOGLE TRUSTS YOUR BRAND MORE WHEN USERS SEARCH FOR YOU BY NAME

In Google's early days, its algorithm had little visibility into how visitors found a website or what they did when they got there. Beginning with the introduction of Google Analytics in 2005 and capped by the unveiling of Google Search Console in 2018, Google now analyzes more information about web traffic than any other company. And it does this in real time, twenty-four hours a day, seven days a week.

All this information is fed into Google's algorithm to improve search experience.

The more engagement and interest in your site, the more Google trusts your brand. One key measure of this engagement is the number of visitors who search for your website by name.

A *branded search* is a Google query that includes the name of your company, product, or brand. It can be a simple search for your brand name ("Idea Grove," in the case of my agency) or a *brand-plus-keyword* query that combines a brand name with a generic keyword or phrase (such as, "Idea Grove PR agency").

Ninety of the Top One Hundred Google Searches Are Branded

Would you be surprised if I told you that ninety of the top one hundred US Google search queries in June 2022 were branded searches? Led by "facebook," "youtube," and "amazon," branded searches also accounted for nine of the top ten Google queries, with only the non-branded keyword "weather" breaking in at #4, according to Ahrefs.

For every "restaurants near me" (ranked #20), there's a "mcdonalds" (#33), "chick fil a" (#48), "pizza hut" (#66), "taco bell" (#71), and "chipotle" (#86). And those branded searches deliver a strong trust signal to Google's algorithm. The more visitors a website gets from branded searches, the more SEO authority Google bestows on the brand.

Brand-plus-keyword searches may be even more powerful because Google looks at searches that combine your brand name with keywords to assess the topics and industries in which you have the most authority. According to research by *Backlinko*, Google may give your website a rankings boost for that keyword as a result—even when your brand name is not included in the search (Dean 2021).

#10: Click-Through Rate (CTR)

Google analyzes the percentage of people who click on a link to your website after seeing it in search results. The higher the CTR, the higher the trust.

#11: Website Visitor Engagement

Individual visitors are influenced by the quality of your site's content and navigation. Google factors in their collective experience by monitoring the average time visitors spend on your site before leaving, along with other engagement metrics.

#12: Social Media Engagement

Individual visitors will be more likely to trust you if you have recent activity on social channels. Google goes deeper, analyzing how much engagement you receive on sites ranging from LinkedIn to Twitter to Glassdoor.

THE ULTIMATE ARBITER OF TRUST

It's probably fair to say that Google's relentlessly expanding algorithm will one day be smarter than all of us. Maybe it already is, given that, over the past quarter century, it has graduated from analyzing fewer than ten million web pages to hundreds of billions today.

That's not quite the googol (10^{100}) of pages that Larry Page and Sergey Brin had in mind when they named their company, but it's heading in that direction. And it has indexed all this information to create an ever-improving formula for determining how, and what, we trust on the web.

That's why I describe Google as the world's ultimate arbiter of trust.

TURNING SIGNALS INTO SOLUTIONS

Over the past four chapters, we have discussed and provided examples of each of the primary kinds of trust signals.

Specifically, we've outlined:

- **twenty-nine types of website trust signals,** ranging from third-party trust seals to professional design and quality content;
- **twenty types of inbound trust signals,** including the major forms of third-party validation to be found online; and
- **twelve types of SEO trust signals,** the hidden clues Google uses to determine where to rank you in search results.

This overview has covered only a portion of the many trust signals your buyers and other audiences use to determine whether to do business with your brand. On my website at TrustSignals. com, I've shared advice on over one hundred trust signals, and I'm adding more all the time.

After a recent presentation on trust signals for Texas Security Bank, I was asked by a member of the audience: "There are so many trust signals. Where should I put my focus? Where should I start?"

While I've tried to include the most important trust signals in the previous chapters, the best way to integrate these signals into your PR and marketing strategy is not as a checklist to be completed. It should be part of a plan. Trust signals should be deployed strategically to help you achieve a business goal.

That's why I developed the Grow With TRUST system. It's designed to put trust signals to work for you in the most focused and effective way possible. We'll be walking through this framework and its components in the latter half of this book.

But first, let's take a closer look at the *impact* trust signals can have on building your brand and growing your business when used successfully.

CHAPTER 8

Trust Signals, Conversions, and Growth

→ Research shows that trust signals can make the difference between success and failure for ecommerce stores.

→ Beyond their impact on online sales, trust signals can help any business build, grow, and protect its brand over time.

→ Measurement of branded search traffic, media share of voice, search presence, and survey data can be used to track increases in brand trust.

E verybody claims to be a growth hacker these days—at least if you check out people's bios on LinkedIn.

The truth is that while marketers, developers, and product managers can team up on some clever customer acquisition strategies to build user bases fast, most things that last take time.

Trust, for example.

You can't build it overnight because until you have some skins on the wall, and until you have proven you are good at what you do, people will be wary. That's just human nature.

One of the things I find most frustrating as a marketer is when companies *do* put in the time and effort to make customers happy—but then don't take the necessary steps to use that accumulated trust to fuel customer acquisition.

It's amazing how many brands have achieved high customer satisfaction levels, industry endorsements, and other trust signals, but simply don't realize the value of sharing this information. Or they understand the value, but they don't know how to effectively share trust signals on their website and in other marketing channels.

You don't need growth hacking in these cases. You simply need to put trust signals to work for your business.

THE INFLUENCE OF WEBSITE TRUST SIGNALS
ON ECOMMERCE SALES

Because trust signals emerged from the world of ecommerce, it shouldn't be surprising that most published research has focused on their impact on conversions and sales. And there is a significant accumulation of data to show that trust signals work.

The Baymard Institute, a user-experience research house based in Denmark, has conducted more than 88,000 hours of studies, tests, and experiments to identify best practices for ecommerce website design. The research covers many of the trust signals we discussed in Chapter 5, including the impact of quality content, intuitive navigation, case studies, first-party reviews, expert endorsements, trust seals, and more.

Following is a sample of what Baymard has learned in its research (Baymard Institute, n.d.).

Quality Content

Baymard found that nearly a third of shoppers consider better product information the most important reason to shop online compared to physical stores, where consumers are often limited to information on product packaging or what a store employee can tell them. Baymard found that online shoppers sought product descriptions that:

- provided comprehensive detail on features, functionalities, materials, and ingredients;
- featured section headings, text blocks, bullet lists, and product highlights that made them easier to read; and
- avoided both technical jargon and flowery, superlative-laden sales copy in describing the product.

When not provided with enough detail, shoppers figured a product didn't have the features they needed—so they left.

If the copy did have enough detail but wasn't organized to be easy to read, the shoppers felt overwhelmed—so they left.

If the copy had sufficient detail and was well-organized, but was too salesy, shoppers felt distrustful—so they left.

Users routinely told Baymard's researchers before abandoning a site that they would "go to Google" to get their questions answered. Many of those users never came back.

Intuitive Navigation

Navigation is important for all websites, but for ecommerce websites offering a wide range of products, mistakes can make the difference between success and failure.

In user studies covering thousands of home page and category navigation elements, Baymard found that subpar user experiences were frustratingly common. The research house reported, for example, that the majority of ecommerce websites required their visitors to use the exact same language the site used when searching for products.

For example, a visitor to an online retailer might search for a blow dryer but not find it if the site used the term "hair dryer" in its taxonomy. That can lead to both the loss of a sale and the assumption that the store doesn't carry the product—causing long-term brand damage.

Ecommerce stores with intuitive navigation, by contrast, increased their sales while burnishing their brands.

Customer Reviews

First-party reviews are customer reviews that a company collects on its own website to share with visitors. Baymard said the importance of these reviews for online shoppers is difficult to overstate—with up to 95 percent of test subjects relying on reviews in their buying decisions.

However, first-party reviews were generally greeted with more skepticism than reviews on Google or other third-party platforms. If a user only found five-star reviews on a brand's website, they were more likely to assume the reviews were manipulated and discount their value.

Baymard found that 53 percent of users specifically sought out bad reviews. Brands that included negative reviews on their site—even allowing users to search for them by star rating—were more trusted by users. Brands also earned trust by responding empathetically, rather than defensively, to negative reviews.

TRUST SEALS:

TRANSLATING TRUST INTO CONVERSIONS

A trust seal provides valuable third-party validation for those websites that use it. But how can this value be measured, and how does it translate into conversions and sales?

TrustedSite, a San Francisco-based web security company and issuer of trust seals, has a longstanding blog series called "Testing Trust," in which digital marketing agencies put its trustmarks to the test for their clients and share their findings (TrustedSite, n.d.).

Some of the results:

- Holabird Sports, a running and racquet sports retailer, saw a 21.3 percent increase in revenue after adding trustmarks on its landing and product pages, login, footer, cart, and checkout.
- Decor Steals, a home furnishings retailer, achieved a 17 percent increase in revenue per desktop visitor after installing trustmarks across its site.

- Scrubs & Beyond, which sells scrubs and medical equipment, recorded an 18.6 percent increase in conversions after adding trustmarks.
- AmourPrints, a retailer of romantic canvas art and prints, saw an 8.6 percent increase in conversions.
- JINS Eyewear, which sells prescription glasses online, experienced an 8.4 percent conversion increase.

Major retail brands don't have the same need for trust seals as smaller ecommerce stores. Brands that are household names generally don't bother displaying the Norton or Better Business Bureau seals on their sites, for example. These brands have established enough trust over time that visitors already believe their businesses are credible and assume their websites are secure.

However, the Baymard Institute notes in its research that design bugs are a frequent cause for cart abandonment for even the largest brands—Amazon, Walmart, and Apple.

The research house gave the example of a flaw in the Microsoft Store's credit-card form that caused placeholder text in the postal code field to be superimposed by the user's auto-fill text. The mistake made the field unreadable. Confused shoppers feared the form did not function properly or had been hacked—so they left.

This example shows that website trust signals, such as professional design and attention to detail, aren't just for smaller brands. Even the biggest brands can lose business through design oversights and other errors that reduce buyer trust.

FROM SHORT-TERM SALES TO LONG-TERM GROWTH

Trust signals clearly help online brands—from apparel retailers to SaaS vendors—to sell more product. But this only scratches the surface of their potential impact over time.

By approaching trust signals more broadly, any business can develop a strategy that improves more than checkout-page conversions. The more far-reaching and enduring benefit of a trust signals strategy is to build, grow, and protect your brand.

I saw a business cartoon recently that made me laugh, then grimace. It showed two men standing in side-by-side kiosks with signs advertising their competing services. One vendor's sign said, "LOW-QUALITY LEADS." The other read, "BRAND BUILDING."

The punchline was that the line for buying bad leads was a mile long. Not a soul was in line to build their brand.

It's a common story, particularly for midsize and smaller companies that believe they simply can't afford the luxury of brand marketing if they want to grow. Unfortunately, this approach often results in businesses that find themselves on a hamster wheel, constantly chasing short-term sales rather than investing in long-term growth.

LEAD GENERATION VERSUS TRUST GENERATION

Brand building is not lead generation. It's *trust* generation. It makes your leads better and your funnel stronger. It can help you avoid commoditization and demand a higher price. It can make the difference in attracting and retaining top talent as well.

I've worked with many CMOs whose narrow focus on MQLs and SQLs (marketing- and sales-qualified leads, respectively) has mostly led to LQLs—*low-quality leads*. Those are the leads that are often a source of friction and finger-pointing between marketing and sales.

Even in the best of circumstances, leads that don't convert are not uncommon. The average MQL—a lead that has shown some level of interest in your product—only becomes an SQL—an actual sales prospect—about 10–15 percent of the time, on average, for most medium- and high-consideration purchases. That's true whether these purchases are B2B or B2C.

But the conversion rate varies greatly based on the quality of the MQL. And while businesses may look at any number of reasons for leads being of low quality—especially from sources like email campaigns and trade shows—the biggest reason is that companies haven't built sufficient brand equity to win their buyers' trust.

The illustration below shows the influence of brand trust on the sales and marketing funnel, adapted from a concept developed by *Branding Strategy Insider*. There are four stages from product awareness to the buying decision—with brand trust, once established, reducing friction all along the journey.

Brand Trust Accelerates the Marketing Funnel

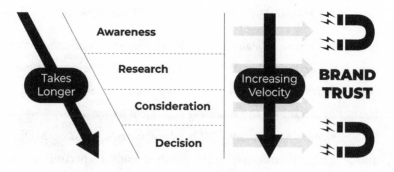

This is how a forward-looking PR firm should view its role in helping companies grow. Don't settle for the limited role of the traditional PR firm, but don't be coaxed by prospects into a short-term, lead-generation focus. Instead, go deeper to help your clients better understand their customers, build awareness, and develop relationships of trust across every marketing touchpoint.

While the value of brand trust can be difficult to measure, one approximation comes in the form of the *goodwill* line of a business's balance sheet. When one company acquires another for a price higher than net fair value, the difference is called "goodwill." The acquired company's brand equity is one of the key components of goodwill.

Today, more than half of the corporations in the S&P 500 have goodwill balances of more than $10 billion from their acquisitions. That's a lot of money paid for brand trust.

AVOIDING THE COFFEE-SPOON APPROACH TO BRAND MEASUREMENT

When T.S. Eliot's J. Alfred Prufrock famously laments that he has "measured out my life with coffee spoons," he is expressing regret for all the opportunities he has lost by leading a safe, predictable life.

So it often goes with brand-building programs. Scrutinizing short-term costs too closely can come at the expense of long-term ambitions. Put another way, if you measure your ROI in coffee spoons, you may end up bemoaning lost opportunities just as Prufrock did.

For this reason, some businesses choose not to measure their investment in brand awareness and growth at all.

In 2021, Lessonly, a successful sales-training platform, was acquired by Seismic, a three-billion-dollar sales-enablement technology company. In celebrating the acquisition on LinkedIn and Twitter, Lessonly CMO Kyle Lacy (2021) shared that one of the keys to the company's growth and success was its decision to "cease all measurement of branding efforts."

Lacy went on to explain that the company decided to split its marketing spend into two parts: demand and brand. While the demand-generation budget was closely measured for ROI, the brand-building spend—representing up to 30 percent of the total marketing budget—wasn't measured at all.

As a result of this decision, Lacy said, "our brand story grew stronger and made a larger impact because it wasn't being constantly scrutinized for spend." The team was able to focus entirely on improving brand awareness and trust rather than constantly worrying about ROI.

Over time, he concluded, this led to greater ambitions, higher returns, and superior growth.

MEASURING THE IMPACT OF TRUST SIGNALS ON BRAND GROWTH

While it's not necessary to go to the lengths of Lessonly, it is crucial not to attempt to tie branding programs directly to sales on a day-to-day basis. That dooms your efforts to failure.

But there are metrics to help you see if you're on the right track in building awareness and trust for your brand through trust signals. These include:

- direct and branded search traffic,
- media visibility and share of voice,
- search and social media presence, and
- market surveys and qualitative research.

Let's take a closer look at each of these metrics.

Direct and Branded Search Traffic

Direct traffic is when someone enters your URL directly into a browser's address bar or clicks on a bookmarked link. Branded search traffic is traffic that results from a Google search for your brand name or brand-plus-keyword combination. A steady increase in direct traffic, branded search traffic, or both is a clear sign that your brand marketing efforts are working.

For one of Idea Grove's clients, an international provider of back-office automation solutions, our team increased media coverage by more than 700 percent in the first year of the engagement. This led directly to a 180 percent increase in direct and branded search traffic to the client's website, a clear indicator that our brand awareness efforts were working.

Media Visibility and Share of Voice

PR agencies have long measured the volume, quality, and tone of media coverage to track increases in media visibility and positive media coverage. Since the 1940s, agencies have used a metric called

Ad Value Equivalency (AVE) to estimate what a media placement would have cost had it been a paid ad, based on a publication's going advertising rates.

Today, PR software vendors like Meltwater offer a modern take on AVE by partnering with website traffic analytics partners like Similarweb. Other measurement companies, like CoverageBook, take a different approach to measuring media visibility—aggregating and reporting on online readership, domain authority, coverage views, links from coverage, and social shares.

If your business has specific industry rivals in its sights, improvements in your brand's Share of Voice (SOV) can be a valuable measure of progress in gaining market awareness and trust. Monitoring tools like Cision and Meltwater can help you track your brand's visibility in the news media and social media relative to competitors.

Search and Social Media Presence

How can you tell if you are building brand trust through your search and social media presence? For me, it was when the phone started ringing.

Shortly after I started Idea Grove as a one-man agency in 2005 I began writing a blog—mostly because I had no clients and nothing better to do with my time! I wrote about whatever came to mind— PR, marketing, technology, movies, celebrity gossip. Anything to keep me, and eventually my audience, amused.

I didn't know much about SEO at the time, but within a few months of starting the blog, I began receiving calls from companies who wanted to work with me. As it turns out, I was one of only a handful of PR practitioners in Texas who were blogging at the time, and Google rewarded me by ranking my agency at the top of search results for terms like "Dallas PR firms"—over giant firms with Dallas offices like Edelman and FleishmanHillard. And the business flowed in.

More than a decade and a half later, it's not as easy as it used to be, because there's a lot more competition. But it still works the same way, and it's still worth it. Increasing your organic search volume, social media engagement, and social media referral traffic is a sure sign you are growing your audience and building trust.

Buyer Surveys and Market Research

Many companies I've worked with—even large ones with sizable marketing budgets—seem to be allergic to conducting market and customer surveys. The cost and time involved scares them off.

That's unfortunate, because this research, done well, is the most precise way to measure your success in building brand awareness. Unlike other sources of measurement, surveys don't require you to make assumptions based on website traffic or other data. There's simply no better way to determine if your brand messaging is hitting its mark or falling on deaf ears than by asking the people you're trying to reach.

Effective research doesn't have to break the bank. You could have questionnaires on your website, asking how visitors discovered you or if they have heard of you before. You could ask your current customers when and how they learned about your brand. You could field surveys of target audiences to see whether they know your brand, and if they do, what they think of it. Do the research in regular intervals, with the same targets, and you'll get a very clear indication of whether your brand-building efforts are working.

BRAND LIFT FOR THE LONG HAUL

Compared to lead-generation programs, it can be very difficult to trace business results directly to specific brand-building efforts. If someone comes across your company's name in a news article, for example, it might result in a branded search weeks later.

Over time, however, if you don't begin to see significant lift in these metrics, it could be a sign that your brand's message isn't resonating or that your product isn't capturing the public's interest. It could also be a sign that your trust signals strategy is missing the mark.

Growth hackers pride themselves on launching clever promotions to grow customer bases fast. But for most brands, a strategy focused on establishing trust—sending the right trust signals to the right audiences at the right time—will deliver better long-term results.

In our post-truth world, figuring out what's "right" for our audiences can be challenging, of course—but it's attainable. We'll tackle that in the next chapter.

CHAPTER 9

Choosing the Right Trust Signals in a Post-Truth World

→ Trust signals are not one size fits all; the signals that work best vary based on your audience.

→ With so many trust signals to choose from, brands must use research to identify those that best align with their goals.

→ Trust profiles are a PR analog to buyer personas in marketing, designed to illuminate what makes audiences trust.

A n ancient Latin proverb offers some good advice about priorities: "*Duos insequens lepores neutrum capit.*"

He who chases two hares catches neither.

In today's world, marketers and business owners are faced with a seemingly unlimited number of rabbits to chase—and an equal number of rabbit holes to avoid.

It would be easy enough if our post-truth world consisted of one audience that watched CNN and another that preferred Fox News. The tougher challenge is that every audience's attention is spread across many sources of information and influence.

Without carefully prioritizing the trust signals you send, you risk spending unlimited marketing dollars to achieve limited results—and sometimes no results at all.

Let's take the issue of information sources. To use your budget wisely, it's critical to gain an understanding of:

- the media outlets that matter to your audience,
- the influencers that affect their decision-making, and
- the review sites your buyers visit and trust.

Faced with these questions, you could do what many marketers do—nod your head impatiently and say, "We'll figure that out with A/B testing. We'll eliminate what fails and double up on what works."

WHY CUSTOMER RESEARCH SAVES YOU
MONEY IN THE LONG RUN

You could do that, but it would cost you—probably far more than the research you have decided to skip.

Specifically:

Media Coverage

It can cost thousands of dollars in agency time to achieve one high-profile media placement. Shouldn't you make sure you've targeted the right source?

Influencers

Whether paid or unpaid, influencers require an investment of time and money. And choosing the wrong ones can actually hurt your brand.

Review Sites

Which review sites should you prioritize? You can't ask your customers to leave reviews for you in six different places. You have to focus on the sources that move the needle.

Think about my friend David, from the breakfast meeting. His company had landed ten million dollars in venture capital. It had happy customers. It had a story to tell. And yet, despite spending a sizable retainer with a PR agency for a year, the startup saw only a modest increase in brand awareness and trust.

Why?

Mostly because the company and agency both assumed that securing media coverage in high-profile outlets—no matter how difficult or time-consuming these placements were to achieve—was the startup's best PR investment. If David's startup had hired an agency that focused not just on media coverage but on that coverage's ultimate purpose—securing trust at scale—the engagement might have gone differently.

But only if the brand first conducted research to determine which trust signals would have the greatest impact.

KNOWING WHO YOU ARE AND WHAT YOUR
AUDIENCES WANT FROM YOU

Trust Signals is a book about brand *building*, not brand *creation*. Having said that, before we dive into research strategies to identify the best trust signals to grow your brand, now might be a good time for you to do a gut check on a fundamental question:

Do you know who you are?

In this book, we discuss universal truths about branding, such as the importance of authenticity, quality, and consistency in sharing your story. But what that means specifically is different for every brand. Be sure you have created a solid brand narrative before sharing it with your audiences if you want to earn their trust.

Knowing who your company is as a brand means being able to look in the mirror and answer these questions, among others:

- What is the core benefit you deliver to buyers?
- What is the personality of your brand?
- How do you differentiate yourself in the market?
- How do you describe yourself to the market?
- How do you make the world a better place?

Once you are confident about who you are, you can use trust signals to tell your story to the world.

DECIDING WHICH TRUST SIGNALS TO PURSUE
AND SHOWCASE

As important as trust signals are, they are not universal in their appeal. What resonates with one audience may not resonate with another.

That's why achieving brand trust is a far more complex undertaking now than it was in the past. In this cancel-culture world, the stakes are higher, too.

Decisions about which trust signals to pursue and showcase, and which to avoid or ignore, shouldn't be made lightly. Calibrate them carefully for risk versus reward.

Questions to ask yourself include:

- Who are my brand's core audiences?
- What values do they share?
- What sources of information do they trust?
- What stances or sources might alienate them?
- What is their trust breadcrumb path?

To answer these questions, it's not enough to gather a group of executives in a boardroom, compile their conjectures on a whiteboard, and call it a strategy. You must first conduct research to ensure your trust-building plan is a solid one.

During this research, your objective is to discover what messages and sources inspire trust, as well as *dis*trust, in your buyers and other audiences.

Their answers may surprise you.

MOVING FROM SMALL TALK TO REAL CONVERSATIONS

Have you ever been to a party where you didn't know anyone? What was that first conversation like? If it's anything like my experiences, it was awkward—a lot of small talk, uncomfortable pauses, and questions asked out of courtesy rather than curiosity.

Compare that to a gathering where everyone already knows each other. Those parties are fun. The conversations are meaningful. The interactions are memorable.

If, as a brand, you haven't taken the time to get to know your buyers, you are perpetually at that first party. You're sending out marketing messages and hoping for a response. Maybe you'll hit on something that resonates. But more likely the buyer will simply flash a polite smile and find someone more interesting to talk to.

How can you avoid that—and get to that second party? The best way to start is with buyer persona research.

CONDUCTING BUYER PERSONA RESEARCH

A *buyer persona* is a semi-fictional representation of your ideal customer based on research into your existing buyers. It encompasses demographics, behavior patterns, motivations, and goals.

My agency, Idea Grove, conducts a range of research and strategy projects for our clients, including brand audits, competitive analyses, go-to-market plans, and more. But the research we do most often is to help our clients create buyer personas.

Idea Grove uses a methodology based on the work of Adele Revella, founder of the Buyer Persona Institute and author of *Buyer Personas: How to Gain Insight into Your Customer's Expectations, Align your Marketing Strategies, and Win More Business*, one of the best business books of the past decade. If you haven't read it, I encourage you to do so.

Consistent with Revella's approach, our team conducts Zoom or phone interviews with recently added contacts in our clients' CRMs—some who ended up purchasing our client's product, others who chose a competitor, and still others who chose not to buy at all.

P roblem

R esults

O bstacles

B uyer's Journey

E valuation

We call our approach PROBE, and it's designed to elicit the following information:

Problem: What was the pain point or problem the buyer hoped to solve?

Results: What results did the buyer expect to see from purchasing the product?

Obstacles: What concerns or objections did the buyer have during the process?

Buyer's Journey: How did the buyer find out about the product and what were the stages in the buying process?

Evaluation: What factors led to the buyer's final decision?

It's difficult to overstate how much our clients have benefited from this research over the years. It has inspired brands to overhaul their marketing strategies, redesign their websites, update their messaging, or make other important changes to better align with buyers.

STUNNING RESULTS, VALUABLE INSIGHTS

Consider the example of one of our clients, a managed service provider (MSP) offering IT consulting services in multiple markets. The MSP was struggling to differentiate itself in its heavily crowded space and asked for our help.

We quickly learned that it was nearly impossible to distinguish our client's website from those of its competitors. They mostly consisted of laundry lists of services and capabilities, along with tired marketing appeals touting the benefits of outsourcing IT for small businesses.

Then, we began doing buyer persona interviews for this client. *What we found was stunning.*

None of the information on the company's website was of particular interest to those we talked to; in fact, there was frustration over the technical jargon and lack of transparency about pricing. But what made these buyers choose our client came shining through—it was their high-touch service, which stood apart in this highly commoditized space.

As one respondent told us:

> They actually got to know us during the sales process. I liked the stories they shared. They seem to like visiting their clients at their offices. Everybody else I talked to was cold by comparison; they insisted they could do everything remotely. Honestly, the other guys sounded like they'd consider the engagement a success if they never had to meet us at all.

This insight led to a complete overhaul of the brand's website, in which we put personal interactions, case studies, and experiences —rather than speeds and feeds—front and center.

You'll recall we discussed in Chapter 5 the power of custom photography as a website trust signal. The warm and intimate shoot we did for this client made all the difference in differentiating the brand.

THE LIMITS OF BUYER PERSONAS

The data we gathered in our buyer interviews helped us determine which trust signals to prioritize. In addition to the custom photography, we added case studies in which long-time customers told candid, sometimes humorous stories of their experiences with the company's employees.

And rather than spend thousands of words describing the technologies of our client's IT partners (major brands like Microsoft), we simply displayed their logos on the site. That was all visitors really needed to see to trust in our client's competence.

But buyer persona research does have its limitations. While essential, *it is no longer sufficient to build a trust-centered marketing program.*

Why?

Because today's customers care about *more* than your product.

And because buyers aren't the *only* audience whose opinions matter.

Let's explore each of these sea changes in more detail.

SEA CHANGE #1: TODAY'S CUSTOMERS CARE ABOUT MORE THAN YOUR PRODUCT

It's not just about your product's features and benefits anymore. When buyers make purchase decisions, they often factor in whether the brand is one they wish to align with—based on the brand's social purpose, political stances, and other considerations.

These factors fall outside the scope of most buyer persona research. They are also questions that most brands never had to worry about in the past.

Three decades ago, when NBA great Michael Jordan was questioned about his decision not to publicly endorse a Black Democrat for the US Senate in his home state of North Carolina, he swatted away the challenge with the swagger of a chase-down block.

"Republicans buy sneakers, too," the face of the Air Jordan brand famously responded.

Jordan, then twenty-seven, took a bit of heat at the time. But his attitude reflected the stance of most brands in 1990: *stay out of politics.*

Consumers Want Brands to Represent Their Values

Over the past decade, particularly after the election of Donald Trump in 2016, things have changed. Americans routinely call on corporate CEOs to take stands on social issues. With our politics mired in dysfunction and gridlock, millions no longer feel represented in Washington. They are now demanding to be "represented" by their favorite brands.

The global PR agency Edelman has been studying public trust for two decades. For its 2022 Edelman Trust Barometer report, the firm conducted interviews with more than 36,000 respondents across twenty-eight countries in the form of a thirty-minute online survey.

The results were gloomy, as expected, for most public institutions—with one exception: *business.*

According to the report, business has emerged as the most trusted institution, surpassing government, the media, and even nonprofit groups (2022 Edelman Trust Barometer). This tracks with a trend of increasing trust in business in Edelman's studies over several years.

CEOs Are Expected to Step Up

But as Spider-Man's Uncle Ben might say, "With great power comes great responsibility."

According to Edelman's research, about eight in ten respondents want CEOs to speak out on issues such as social injustice. More than two-thirds of respondents expect a CEO to step in to fix a problem when the government refuses to act.

This transformation in public expectations is evident across virtually every business and industry—including Jordan's NBA.

The face of the league today is LeBron James. Unlike Jordan, James is fearless in sharing his values and views. And at thirty-seven, he's already a billionaire—with 30 percent of that wealth coming from his salary and 70 percent from endorsements, entertainment deals, and other non-NBA sources.

LeBron knows his audience. He's built a career off the court by showing his fans *who he is* off the court—creating closer bonds in the process.

Consumers want their favorite brands to represent their values. They will buy from, advocate for, and *trust* those that do. But they will punish those that don't.

A survey of consumers by the B2B review site Clutch demonstrates this clearly:

- Seventy-one percent of respondents said they think it's important for businesses to take a stand on social issues.

- Seventy-five percent said they are likely to start shopping at a company that supports an issue they agree with.

- Fifty-nine percent said they are likely to stop shopping at a company that supports an issue they disagree with.

- Respondents ranked social responsibility as a more important attribute of a brand than price.

Buyer persona research is typically not geared to address this broader universe of motivations.

SEA CHANGE #2: BUYERS AREN'T THE ONLY AUDIENCE WHOSE OPINIONS MATTER

Recall how the writer for PRSA's (2015) *PRsay* blog described the difference between marketing and PR:

> Marketing addresses consumers of a product or service. Public relations is the strategic function that addresses all of an organization's key constituencies.

Buyer persona research is a marketing tool. Its name alone explains who it's designed for—buyers. Not investors, employees, suppliers, partners, or community activists.

Not too long ago, most brands—particularly midsize and smaller businesses—didn't worry much about "constituencies" other than their customers.

Who had time to, after all? And what constituencies did they really need to worry about?

Even Small Companies Must Consider Non-Customer Audiences

Sure, all companies had to take care of their employees. But broader concerns like corporate social responsibility, investor relations, political activism, crisis communications, and community outreach? Those were for the big, not the *bit*, players.

That's no longer the case. No company, of any size, can afford to ignore their non-customer audiences and the impact they can have on their brand.

I get my hair cut at a neighborhood salon in Dallas. Some time back, the salon began getting dozens of vicious phone calls—and one-star reviews—from people all over the country. Why? Because people had confused the salon's name with that of another local parlor, whose owner had been weighing in on controversial issues on social media.

My salon was able to clear up the confusion and live to tell the tale—but they learned the hard way that their world now extends well beyond the people sitting in their styling chairs.

TRUST PROFILES: PR'S ANSWER TO BUYER PERSONAS

Buyer personas are by and for marketers. That's their strength and also their limitation.

The issue of trust—extending to non-product concerns and non-customer audiences—is a PR issue. And it needs a PR solution rooted in research.

My recommended solution is the *trust profile*.

The trust profile is a PR analog to the buyer persona. The goal of a trust profile is to help brands understand what inspires trust (and *dis*trust) in their audiences, in the same way that buyer personas shed light on customers and the buying process.

My hope is that PR practitioners will embrace this kind of research as their responsibility—and that as such, they will become the *keepers of trust* for brands. PR people should make it our business to understand the "prejudices and symbols and cliches and verbal formulas" that make people tick, as Edward Bernays had envisioned.

One PR agency, the billion-dollar global firm Edelman, has taken steps in this direction.

In addition to its annual Trust Barometer survey, the agency has launched the Edelman Trust Management practice, as well as the Edelman Trust Institute, to conduct research and consult with clients on brand trust.

"Society is at an inflection point," the institute's chairman said upon its launch in 2021, "and we believe that trust is a defining business metric for companies and brands" (Edelman 2021).

Unfortunately, conducting custom research into brand trust with Edelman is financially out of reach for the vast majority of companies. But these businesses still need insight into what makes audiences tick—and trust.

THE BLIND LEADING THE BLIND

If I've heard the question once, I've heard it a thousand times:

So, which publications would you like to be featured in?

That's what PR firms typically ask their new clients by way of "research."

They might as well say:

We don't know your audience, where they consume information, or who they trust. Can you tell us?

And most clients don't know the answer to the question, either.

What PR should be doing is actual research—enough to develop and present a plan. As in:

These are the sources of third-party validation your target market seeks out and trusts. Focus your efforts on these three things.

Because when data is lacking, superficial goals, like getting the CEO in *Forbes* to feed his ego, tend to become the "strategy." Or worse.

I was once approached by a prospective client that had a great story to tell—one I believed could earn widespread media attention. Unfortunately, the CEO already had a very specific goal in mind: he wanted to be on Fox News and Fox Business— and nowhere else.

The CEO had no real basis for this decision, and certainly no research to support it. He was simply a conservative Republican who truly believed the only credible major news networks were owned by Fox. The rest were "fake news"—and he didn't want to be associated with them.

Needless to say, the CEO's PR plan was doomed from the start. Because it isn't what *he* believes is fake or real that matters; it is what his buyers and other audiences believe.

And that can only be determined through research.

HOW TO BUILD A TRUST PROFILE

While every brand's needs are different, here's a three-step approach to building a trust profile that will work for most companies:

1. Determine which audiences are important to you.
2. Perform sentiment-and-language analysis to understand how these audiences talk and think.
3. Conduct quantitative surveys to understand your audiences' values, views, and trusted information sources.

Let's explore each of these steps.

Step #1: Determine Which Audiences Are Important to You

Most senior PR professionals report to the CMO or vice president of marketing for a simple reason. For most brands, the customer is far and away the most important audience.

But today, other audiences are critically important as well. Amid the pandemic-driven Great Resignation, many of my agency's clients told us that their biggest issue wasn't sales; it was recruiting. They were having to turn away customers because they didn't have enough people to do the work.

These brands understand that raising awareness and building trust with job seekers—and making advocates of their employees—can make or break their business.

So it is with other audiences, such as investors. Whether your brand is a public company, a startup looking for VC money, or a small business seeking a loan, your reputation precedes you—and adds to or subtracts from the bottom line.

For tech brands, channel partners might be your lifeblood. For local service businesses, a visible presence in local communities is key. Identify your most important audiences—then get to work understanding what makes them trust.

Step #2: Analyze How Your Audiences Talk and Think

A decade ago, IBM famously estimated that 90 percent of the world's data had been created in the previous two years—2.5 quintillion bytes of data every day. The accumulation of data online, including millions of tweets, Facebook comments and TikTok videos, has only accelerated since then (Bhambhri 2012).

That's a gold mine of information—if you know what you're looking for.

I've referred several times now to this quote from Edward Bernays, because it was so prescient when he wrote it in 1928:

> Modern business must have its finger continuously on the public pulse. The voice of the people expresses the mind of the people...composed of inherited prejudices and symbols and cliches and verbal formulas... (Propaganda)

Before diving into quantitative surveys, I recommend putting your finger on the pulse of your target audiences by using AI tools to sort through the treasure trove of relevant data already online. Sentiment-and-language analysis is the kind of research Bernays could only dream of—and it's become increasingly accurate and affordable.

Social media listening software that detects when your brand is mentioned positively or negatively online is one of the most common forms of sentiment analysis. Tools can analyze your media coverage for positive or negative tone as well.

But building a trust profile requires going deeper than that. You need to understand how your audiences talk and what's important to them.

At Idea Grove, for example, one of our resources is software that analyzes the words and language that brand audiences use in customer reviews, on Twitter, in online forums, and elsewhere. This helps us understand how audiences *talk* about our clients' brands relative to their competitors—while surfacing the words, phrases, and ideas that resonate most.

Among its many uses, this information is invaluable for creating a website that makes your visitors feel at home. If your content reads like your visitors talk, chances are they'll step right in and stay a while.

WHAT BRAIN SCANS TELL US
ABOUT TRUST

Marketers have begun to explore the use of neuroimaging—functional MRI brain scans—in determining what trust signals have the biggest impact on specific audiences.

In 2019, academics Luis-Alberto Casado-Aranda, Angelika Dimoka, and Juan Sánchez-Fernández published a study, in the *Journal of Interactive Marketing,* in which they used neuroimaging to compare the reaction of online shoppers to website trust signals ("Consumer Processing of Online Trust Signals").

The researchers tested three types of signals:

1. Trust seals

2. Star ratings based on customer feedback

3. Vendor "assurance statements"

The study, conducted at the University of Granada in Spain, monitored twenty-nine shoppers in the purchase process for a book. They were shown the Confianza Online security trust seal; a ratings table featuring five-star and near five-star ratings for the bookseller; and statements by the bookseller providing assurances on shipping, privacy, and security.

The research showed that trust seals were the most trusted by shoppers and the star ratings least, with assurance statements somewhere in the middle. The report stated that "third-party certificates are far more trustworthy than rating systems given the activation in previously hypothesized ventral striatum and septal areas."

Translation: the Confianza Online security seal activated parts of the brain showing trust, while the star ratings activated parts of the brain revealing feelings of ambiguity and risk. Interestingly, this is despite the fact that in an accompanying survey, the study participants rated these trust signals as virtually identical in influence.

Previous neuroimaging research has tested the impact of variables like pricing and website usability on shopper trust.

As the cost of neuroimaging has come down in recent years, studies of this kind represent a feasible way for marketers to compare a specific audience's reactions to different potential trust signals—and to get more accurate results than a survey might yield.

Step #3: Survey Your Audiences to Reveal Their Values and Views

Unlike with buyer persona research, it's impossible to build a trust profile based exclusively on qualitative data.

The reason is simple. Buyer personas are about finding the common threads that drive your customers' purchase decisions. Brands rarely need more than two or three personas. Buyer Persona Institute founder Adele Revella argues that the goal of marketers should be to narrow their focus to *a single persona* if possible. That way your marketing dollars can deliver more bang for the buck.

At Idea Grove, it rarely takes us more than eight to ten interviews to identify a brand's buyer personas. By asking the right questions, we are able to identify themes in buyer motivations and goals, obstacles to purchase, and decision criteria fairly quickly. This is consistent with Revella's experience in thousands of interviews she and her team have conducted.

Think of buyer persona research as following a buyer down the marketing funnel and documenting the decisions they make along the way. It's like watching a lab mouse work their way through a maze. The peanut butter or dried banana they discover upon solving the maze is your product or service. Your job is to figure out how they got there, why they went there, and how to replicate and scale that experience.

A trust profile is a different kind of research. You're not following someone's path to purchase. You're not in the funnel with them. You're *above* the funnel—out there where people are just living their lives and not thinking about you at all. What *are* they thinking about? What do they care about? What makes them angry?

What information sources do they rely on in their day-to-day lives?

If you ask eight to ten people these questions in phone interviews, you'll get eight to ten different answers. You won't be able to make heads or tails of it.

But if you survey one thousand or more individuals among your target audiences, patterns will start to develop. The scales will fall from your eyes. And you'll begin to understand how to earn your audiences' trust.

Let's say you are most interested in your customer audience and your employee audience. If you're an established company with a decent-sized customer base, start with the contacts in your CRM. Tell them you want to get to know them better in order to better serve them. Offer them an incentive to participate. Do the same with your recruiting database for your employees and candidate pool.

If the numbers don't add up to be statistically viable, supplement the contacts from your own databases with *lookalike audience builders*. These tools help create target audience lists by identifying social media users with similar characteristics, interests, and behaviors as your existing customers.

Once you have enough contacts, fire off a survey that dives into all the key questions we've covered in this book.

A SAMPLE TRUST PROFILE SURVEY

Without going into too much detail, and recognizing that every brand is different, I want to give you a sense of what a trust profile survey might look like. Here's an excerpt from a survey we conducted with Cygnal, a Washington, D.C.-based political- and market-research firm.

The following statements are about potential attributes of companies, businesses, and other types of organizations. Thinking about the businesses and organizations you come in contact with every day — whether in your personal life or in a work capacity—please indicate how important each of the following attributes are to you.

1 - Very Important / 2 - Somewhat Important / 3 - Neither Important Nor Unimportant / 4 - Somewhat Unimportant / 5 - Very Unimportant / 6 - Unsure

	Question	1	2	3	4	5	6
1	Positive previous personal experience with the organization.						
2	The organization's reputation as reflected by positive media coverage, accomplishments, awards, history, and/or financial success.						
3	The organization's stated social values or participation in causes that align with my own social values.						
4	The organization's stated political views and/or political contributions that align with my own political views.						

Still thinking about the businesses and organizations you come in contact with every day, please indicate how much you agree with each of the following statements.

1 - Strongly Agree / 2 - Somewhat Agree / 3 - Neither Agree Nor Disagree / 4 - Somewhat Disagree / 5 - Strongly Disagree / 6 - Unsure

		1	2	3	4	5	6
5	It's important to me that the companies, businesses, and organizations I interact with are outspoken and public about their political and social views.						
6	I research companies to determine their social and political views before working with them.						
7	I research companies to find out how they treat their employees before working with them.						
8	It's important to me that a company has women and minorities in leadership positions.						

	Question	1	2	3	4	5	6
9	A company's social and political views are just as important to me as their ability to get the job done.						
10	Even if I agree with a company's social and/or political views, I'd rather they kept their social and political views to themselves.						
11	I'm offended when non-political organizations push their views on their customers and the public.						

The following is a list of issues and topics that may have been in the news recently. For each one, please indicate how important it is to you that the organizations you come in contact with take a stand on it.

1 - Very Important / 2 - Somewhat Important / 3 - Neither Important Nor Unimportant / 4 - Somewhat Unimportant / 5 - Very Unimportant / 6 - Unsure

12	Black Lives Matter						
13	Climate Change						
14	Immigration						
15	Sustainability						
16	The #MeToo Movement						
17	LGBTQ+ Issues						
18	Traditional Family Values						
19	In a few of your own words, how do you feel when a company in a traditionally non-political space (like an accounting or marketing firm) expresses a strong political or social viewpoint?						
20	In a few of your own words, how do you want to feel about the companies you interact with?						

A survey of this kind can help you understand what your audiences want *before* you develop a social purpose strategy, take a stand on an issue, or respond to social media activism or complaints.

With the same approach, you can ask your target audiences about their trusted (and *dis*trusted) information sources, website trust signals, review sites, and online influencers. Depending on your needs and audience, this research can be performed in a single survey or in a series of surveys conducted over a period of months.

Together with your buyer persona research and AI analysis, you should then have the information necessary to create trust profiles for each of your core audiences that detail the:

- media sources that matter to them,
- influencers and review sites that affect their decision-making,
- issues or stances that attract or alienate them, and
- words and language that resonate with them.

It's everything you need to begin a Grow With TRUST program.

PART 2

Building Your Brand with Trust

CHAPTER 10

The Grow With TRUST System

→ Grow With TRUST is a framework for a more modern, integrated, and comprehensive approach to the practice of PR.

→ TRUST is an acronym representing five PR and marketing solutions: third-party validation, reputation management, user experience, search presence, and thought leadership.

→ The Grow With TRUST system is the best path for virtually any business to build, grow, and protect its brand.

I started Idea Grove at the worst possible time in my life.

I left my last corporate job in the fall of 2004, with the intent to launch my own business in early 2005. But just as that plan was coming together, I was blindsided by a series of tragedies, including my mother's unexpected passing and harrowing health crises for my wife and brother.

I was also jobless—and trying to get a website up for my company and, somehow, find the motivation to win clients and to work.

It felt pretty hopeless. I was just too distracted and depressed.

The one thing I *was* able to do—more as therapy than anything else—was start a blog on the new Idea Grove website.

I'd never owned or worked at an agency before, and I'd never had a blog before, either—very few PR people did at the time. So I decided to just be myself and have fun with it.

I didn't take it too seriously. I had enough things to worry about, after all. I just got by as best I could, taking it a day at a time.

But then several months after I started the blog, something strange and unexpected happened: people started calling who wanted to work with me. They had found my blog in various Google searches or mentioned by other bloggers.

I realized that letting down my guard had drawn people in. When prospects reached out to me for the first time, it was like they already knew me. They knew my personality, my sense of humor, my professional background, and my approach to PR and marketing.

Without realizing it, I had been laying breadcrumbs of trust for Idea Grove through my blog all along.

SUCCESS WITHOUT SELLING

By early 2006 I had a full client load, and the agency has been going strong ever since. Idea Grove has been a three-time Inc. 5000 company and ranked as one of Inc.'s Best Workplaces in 2021 and 2022. We've won our fair share of local and national awards. And most meaningful to me, we've launched the careers of dozens of young PR and marketing professionals.

What I've learned from this experience is that you can be successful without "selling"—if you are able to achieve awareness and trust.

To this day, Idea Grove has earned virtually all its business organically, through PR, referrals, social media, and search.

That's why I believe in the power of trust signals to grow brands. I've seen this, time and again, for Idea Grove's own clients —like the two-person startup we helped to a $100 million exit, or the twenty-something coder with the full-time job who created an Android app in his spare time that we helped to forty million downloads.

Today we work with companies of all sizes, including some of the biggest brands in the world. The Grow With TRUST system is our foundation in helping them build, grow, and protect their brands.

FROM TRUST SIGNALS TO A TRUST SYSTEM

I wrote this book because I believe that trust signals are the tools that should fill every PR professional's tool kit in 2022. A modern public relations agency should be able to help its clients build a path of credibility—breadcrumbs of trust—that accelerates every aspect of the marketing funnel.

But having a list of trust signals to work from isn't enough. Every brand's trust-building efforts should be part of a unified plan. While I've detailed some of the most important trust signals in earlier chapters, the best way to integrate these signals into a PR and marketing program is to organize them strategically, with specific goals in mind.

That's where the Grow With TRUST system comes in. It brings together trust signals in an integrated set of solutions, all designed to help brands secure trust at scale.

The "TRUST" in Grow With TRUST is an acronym for the five PR and marketing solutions I believe every modern PR firm should offer to help their clients secure trust at scale:

T hird-Party Validation

R eputation Management

U ser Experience

S earch Presence

T hought Leadership

These solutions require the use of multiple disciplines to be successful. When all you have is a hammer, all you see are nails, but it's time for forward-looking PR agencies to grab a saw, a screwdriver, and a level, and build trust across all audiences important to their clients.

The five solutions within the Grow With TRUST system each consist of three program strategies. Let's take a closer look at the Grow With TRUST system, solutions, and strategies.

Solution #1: Third-Party Validation

People want to hear what other people say about you, not what you say about yourself. This includes the media, influencers, analysts, experts, and—most importantly—customers.

A third-party validation program should consist of three primary strategies:

1. Media relations strategy
2. Influencer marketing strategy
3. Online review strategy

To build a brand in today's post-truth world, companies must consistently secure third-party validation—and showcase it at every marketing touchpoint.

Solution #2: Reputation Management

It's critical to listen and respond to what customers, employees, and others are saying about you on social media, including sites such as Glassdoor and product review sites.

A reputation management program should consist of three primary strategies:

1. Proactive reputation building
2. Crisis preparation strategy
3. Monitoring and response strategy

Brands must anticipate and prepare for a full range of reputation challenges, including customer criticism, company crises, and social media cancellation attempts.

Solution #3: User Experience

User experience is how your buyers and other audiences interact with your brand in all the spaces you control online—from your website to your social media accounts. Are you creating experiences that build brand trust?

A user experience program should consist of three primary strategies:

1. Trust-centered website design
2. Owned media strategy
3. Full-funnel content strategy

Brands must create compelling, consistent brand experiences across online touchpoints to break through the noise and connect.

Solution #4: Search Presence

Google is not only the world's largest search engine; it's also its most powerful media company. Improving your brand's visibility and trust online starts with your search presence—which tells the world what Google (or at least its algorithms) thinks of your brand.

A search presence program should consist of three primary strategies:

1. Digital PR strategy
2. Technical and on-page SEO strategy
3. Zero-click SEO strategy

PR and SEO have effectively merged in recent years. Not taking an integrated approach to these disciplines is a significant missed opportunity for agencies and brands.

Solution #5: Thought Leadership

Sharing interesting and helpful information with those who come across you online is one of the best ways to build trust with them. It shows you have more to offer the world than a widget to sell.

Your thought leadership program should consist of three primary strategies:

1. Thought leadership platform
2. Contributed content strategy
3. Executive visibility strategy

The bottom line on thought leadership: talk about your ideas more and your products less.

THE CASE FOR A PR-CENTRIC APPROACH
TO DIGITAL MARKETING

The Grow With TRUST system represents the most effective way for virtually any company to build, grow, and protect its brand today. It's also the most natural way for PR agencies to meaningfully differentiate their services from those of other digital marketing firms.

And digital marketing is a field where meaningful differentiation is hard to come by these days.

Think about it.

Over the past decade, virtually every kind of agency has recast itself as a digital marketing firm:

- Agencies that were SEO or PPC specialists have become digital marketing firms.
- Agencies that were web design shops—or even print design shops—have become digital marketing firms.
- Advertising firms that used to make their money from billboards and TV ads have become digital marketing firms.
- And traditional PR firms have become digital marketing firms, too.

That creates a lot of choices for brands—all of which can sound pretty similar when you visit these agencies' websites.

So what's a company in need of digital marketing services to do?

AN AGENCY'S HISTORY MATTERS

When we assess people as individuals—whether it's a job candidate for your company or a romantic interest in your personal life—we tend to do some specific kinds of research. We don't rely on what they tell us during a first interview or a first date. We fire up the Google machine. We study their personal histories and backgrounds.

The same goes for digital marketing agencies. Before you choose one, do a little research into their history. The niche where an agency started typically has a disproportionate influence on its strengths, weaknesses, and strategic focus.

For example:

SEO-Centric Digital Marketing

Until fairly recently, SEO was a highly idiosyncratic field. It operated in a completely separate world from other forms of marketing.

The reason is that the driving rationale for SEO from 1995 to 2010 was to "game" Google—to exploit gaps in algorithms—with link farms, offshore website networks, and other tricks of the trade. "Good SEO" is what an SEO firm would call it when you searched Google for a Boston Kreme and got a corner donut shop in Roxbury instead of Dunkin' Donuts.

Since 2010, Google has been on a systematic, Sherman-like March to the Sea against this kind of SEO—now known as "unnatural" link-building—wiping it out with ruthless efficiency through steady improvements to its algorithm. Many traditional SEO firms have repositioned themselves as digital marketing agencies to adapt to this new reality.

The challenge for these firms is that what Google wants today is what website visitors want: sites that earn their ranking and visibility by generating high-quality content that attracts real audiences, as well as earning links from high-authority sites like news media outlets.

In other words, Google rewards quality today—not trickery.

Many SEO-centered digital marketing firms have had a difficult time making this transition. Their historic focus on collecting backlinks and increasing rankings by any means necessary consigns them to the role of tactical resource rather than strategic partner.

Design-Centric Digital Marketing

Web design firms have been squeezed by easy-to-download WordPress templates and plug-ins that have made building a high-quality website easier than in the past. Making it even tougher for these firms, more clients are asking hard questions about the design process.

Before, creatives could mesmerize clients with talk of how their designs "tap into the energy of your business" or "symbolize movement toward the future." They would talk about color theory and aesthetics, but rarely about the *purpose* of your site: to grow your business. Now, clients expect the proof to be in the pudding. If they are going to spend $50K or more on a website, they want to make sure it will deliver results.

These are the changes that have turned web design firms into digital marketing agencies. But for many design-centric firms—accustomed to being hired for their visual eye rather than KPIs—it has not been an easy transition.

Advertising-Centric Digital Marketing

Many traditional advertising firms have also repositioned themselves as digital marketing agencies. The irony is that inbound marketing is very much a response—a negative one—to the paid, one-way messaging that advertising agencies have specialized in since the days of Don Draper and before.

Today, consumers want genuine dialogue with brands. And they would rather hear from the brand's customers, influencers, and others than the brand itself. While advertising is necessary to amplify the organic reach of digital marketing programs, it is no longer an end in itself.

PR-Centric Digital Marketing

The problem for firms that start with SEO, web design, or advertising as their core discipline is that, while these are all important tools for digital marketers, they are not the foundation for an integrated digital marketing strategy in 2022.

What *is* the foundation?

Telling authentic stories that earn third-party validation organically. That's been the focus of PR for the past one hundred years.

When journalists change careers, it is typically to go into PR because it's such a natural transition. Journalists are less likely to join SEO or web design firms, and when they do, they often feel like fish out of water—a "content provider" bolted onto an agency that doesn't really understand storytelling.

Too often, hiring a firm that is SEO-, design-, or advertising-centric to manage your digital marketing strategy is choosing the tail to wag the dog. You're better off picking an agency that knows how to tell your brand's story in a way that can earn attention—and trust—organically.

Over the next several chapters, we'll outline how the Grow With TRUST system—a PR-centric approach to digital marketing—is the most effective way to build, grow, and protect your brand.

CHAPTER 11

Earning Approval— Third-Party Validation

→ Media coverage in top outlets remains the holy grail for third-party validation—but today it must be amplified to unlock its value.

→ Social media influencers come in all shapes and sizes. Your best results may come from those with small but targeted followings.

→ Customer reviews can make or break your brand. Prioritize the review sites that matter; then, build a five-star presence.

Influencer endorsements didn't begin with the Kardashians' promotion of flat-tummy shakes, hair vitamins, and twenty-five-dollar "couture" lollipops. They go back much further.

One of their earliest uses as trust signals was by British entrepreneur Josiah Wedgwood, who corralled high-profile customers like Queen Charlotte (wife of *Hamilton* favorite George III) to endorse his fine china way back in the 1700s.

Talk about trust seals: a coat of arms accompanied by the words "By Appointment to HRH (Her Royal Highness)" is a pretty good one to have on your advertising.

Whether it's a Kardashian, a queen, or a reviewer on Yelp, people want to hear what other people say about you, not what you say about yourself. That includes the media, influencers, analysts, experts, and—most importantly—your customers.

The elements of third-party validation are inextricably linked today. For example, if Idea Grove's media-relations team pitches a story about a client to one of our media contacts, one of the first things that reporter will do is Google the client to check out its customer reviews and other social proof. Should the journalist decide to write a story, they may feature customer quotes about the client pulled directly from these sites, simply because they don't have time to find and interview customers themselves.

The dynamic is similar with influencer relations. You'll have a much easier time landing the right influencers for your campaign if your business already has good visibility, glowing reviews, and positive coverage online. Image is everything to influencers, after all; the best ones are very careful about who they partner with. They do their research.

STRATEGIES FOR BUILDING TRUST WITH
THIRD-PARTY VALIDATION

We listed twenty forms of third-party validation in Chapter 6, ranging from speaking engagements to Wikipedia pages. But the three key pillars of a third-party validation program are the following:

1. **Media relations strategy.** Securing news media coverage in top outlets is the holy grail for third-party validation and has tremendous value when leveraged correctly.
2. **Influencer marketing strategy.** Social media influencers come in all shapes and sizes. Sometimes your best bets have very small—but highly targeted—followings. Your job is to find them.
3. **Online review strategy.** Customer reviews can make or break your brand online. Prioritize the review sites that matter; then, build a five-star presence.

Let's discuss how to use each of these strategies to construct a successful third-party validation program, starting with media coverage.

Strategy #1: Media Relations

First, let's talk about the wrong way to get media validation.

Scrolling through an Instagram feed today is a lot like driving on the highway and seeing a line of billboards that stretches over the horizon. There are endless ads—often eerily well-targeted.

One ad I've seen many times is for a company called Brand Featured, which targets small businesses and ecommerce stores.

Here's a partial transcript from the video ad (featuring a young spokesmodel who is popular on Fiverr):

> So why aren't people buying? One reason is a lack of trust.
>
> If your website does not have enough five-star reviews or trust elements, visitors won't trust you enough to buy. But if they don't buy, you can't get those five-star reviews in the first place.
>
> This negative loop can stop you from growing your business.
>
> But there's actually a really easy way out of this, and it only takes five minutes to do.
>
> Imagine if on your website you could have the phrase "As Seen On" big news sites like NBC, CBS, FOX, and more. You'd get a huge boost in credibility resulting in more sales for your business.
>
> At Brand Featured, we do exactly that. We'll write an article about your company and publish it to our wide network of over one hundred news sites, including affiliates of NBC, CBS, FOX, and more.
>
> Once your article is published, you'll be able to proudly say, "As Seen On" these authority news sites.

Too Good to Be True

You know what they say: if something sounds too good to be true, it probably is.

What Brand Featured and services like it do is simply distribute a press release that is syndicated across many news sites. Your story has not been *selected* by affiliates of NBC, CBS, or FOX; these sites and others publish thousands of newswire press releases every day. It's an automated service. No one at NBC, CBS, or FOX is reading it or vetting it before it is published—and no credibility is actually conferred.

In fact, there is typically a disclaimer under the headline that says the news outlet "was not involved in the creation of this content."

That's why it "only takes five minutes to do."

Being one of countless companies whose press releases are published daily on news sites, through automated syndication, is not the same as earning media coverage.

And when your website visitors figure out what you're doing (i.e., trying to trade on a media brand's credibility without actually earning it), that can actually become a trust *killer* for your brand.

Earning Media Coverage the Right Way Takes Time

It's understandable why services like Brand Featured exist. Media coverage from well-known outlets confers enormous credibility, even in our fractured, post-truth world. And the better aligned those media sources are with your audience, the stronger the trust signal that coverage will send.

But when it comes to earning meaningful editorial coverage from top media outlets, there's just no getting around it: it's hard work, and it takes time.

It used to be easier. A decade ago, a company could put a press release on the wire, blast it to a massive email list of media targets, and garner coverage. Today, a strategy like that can still work for the Amazons of the world, but for lesser-known brands, the only response you might get from journalists is an "unsubscribe" message.

For all but the biggest brands, media relations today requires a more targeted, thoughtful, and empathetic approach to be successful. Newsrooms are shrinking, writers fresh out of college are replacing industry veterans, reporters are jumping from job to job—and, all the while, those journalists are now juggling numerous topics or "beats," often for multiple outlets. That's a lot of stress and pressure for reporters to deal with.

So start with the premise that your job is to make their job easier by giving them something of value. This requires you to answer a number of questions before you ever send out your pitch:

- What have they written about recently?
- What are they tweeting?
- What angles do they typically take in their stories?
- Do they tend to interview execs? Write trend stories? Prefer data-driven pieces? Incorporate video?

We live in a world where everything is tailored to our preferences; we expect to be given what we want, from the targeted ads in our Instagram feeds to the content recommended to us on Netflix. Reporters expect that, too.

That also means when a journalist *does* bite on your pitch, you better be ready to deliver: with executives on standby, together with all the supporting data and assets necessary for the reporter to write the story. Otherwise, they will lose interest and find another story to chase.

The math is simple. Forty years ago, there was about one PR person for every journalist. By 2010, the ratio stood at four PR people to every journalist. Today, it's a six-to-one ratio and climbing. That means each interaction with a reporter is precious. It also means that it's more important than ever to make sure the media sources you pitch are the right ones—the ones that will send the most powerful trust signals to your target audiences.

Making Sure the Right People See Your Coverage

Once a story is published about your brand, your work shouldn't stop there. The sheer volume of content published today means the feature article secured for you can be quickly buried by several others like it. It falls off the publication's home page and down the list of your industry's Google News results.

That means a smart media relations strategy today must include making sure the right people see your coverage.

How to achieve this? A number of ways, including the following:

- Running targeted ads that point your buyers to the coverage
- Including the coverage in your email marketing
- Guiding your sales team in using the coverage in their prospecting emails
- Sharing your coverage on social media and amplifying it with ads
- Encouraging your employees to share your coverage in their social channels
- Highlighting the media coverage on your company blog
- Creating a search-optimized online newsroom that draws both journalists and buyers to your coverage

And of course, let's not forget adding an "As Seen On" section to your home page, complete with media logos and links to the coverage you've legitimately earned. That's the right kind of website trust signal to send your visitors.

THE SECRET SUPERPOWERS OF MEDIA COVERAGE

Believe me: if the reality of dwindling readership has soured you on the value of earned media, I get where you're coming from. I really do.

But you'd be wrong. Because in many ways, despite the challenges the media industry faces, news coverage in well-known media outlets is a more powerful marketing tool than ever before.

In our fragmented media environment—and in a post-truth world where information sources are under constant scrutiny—established media organizations carry enormous weight where it matters most. And it matters most with Google, YouTube, Facebook, Twitter, and Wikipedia—the most trafficked websites in the world.

Let me explain why.

Google Ranks Sites with Media Coverage Higher

Google is not only a search engine but the most powerful media company in the world, with more than five *billion* (with a "b") visitors per day. These visitors depend on Google to tell them which sites they should visit and what content they should be consuming. And in answering their queries, Google relies heavily on traditional media sources.

To highlight this point, Google's John Mueller has stated that a single high-quality backlink from a major news source is more valuable to your website's search position than "millions" of low-quality backlinks. Mueller added that PR is the most effective, and least spammy, strategy for earning links (Southern 2021).

Facebook and YouTube Are Removing Less-Trusted Sources

Social media sites such as Facebook and YouTube have taken a lot of heat over the past couple of years for their lax moderation of news content—which led to an explosion of fake news. In response to this problem, organizations such as the Trust Project have emerged to help restore integrity to online news.

The Trust Project—endorsed by more than two hundred news organizations including PBS, the BBC, *The Economist*, Hearst, and Sky News—has partnered with Facebook and other social sites to help police the accuracy of online content. This has led to main-stream news sources achieving greater visibility on Facebook.

YouTube, meanwhile, in the past two years has removed tens of thousands of videos for spreading misinformation. Users increasingly expect Facebook and YouTube to take a stand against fake news, which means these sites are relying on traditional media sources more and independent sources less. That means earned media coverage in respected outlets is gaining more exposure and authority with audiences.

Twitter Validates Users Based on Media Coverage

A verified badge on Twitter has long been one of the most coveted status symbols online. Earning that blue checkmark tells the world you're established in your field. But Twitter, like other social media sites that offer verification, has traditionally been less than forthcoming about what makes an account eligible for this designation.

That changed last year, when Twitter unveiled a new verification policy outlining the criteria for obtaining a badge on the platform. To qualify, "your account must be authentic, notable, and active."

Twitter's assessment of notability includes meeting two of these three requirements:

1. Presence in public indices, such as Google Trends, public stock exchanges, or Wikipedia
2. Three or more featured references in the previous six months in media outlets that meet Twitter's criteria for news organizations, including newspapers, magazines, TV, and digital outlets that adhere to journalism standards such as those laid out by the Society of Professional Journalists

3. A follower count in the top 0.05 percent of active accounts located in the same geographic region

Reaching the top 0.05 percent of accounts would be a tough proposition for most businesses. But proving your account is notable through earned media coverage and having a presence in public indices such as Wikipedia is reasonably attainable and the much easier route in securing a blue checkmark next to your brand's name. This underscores the importance of media coverage to attaining social proof.

For Wikipedia, Notability Comes from Media Coverage

In addition to being one of the most visited sites on the internet, Wikipedia is an unrivaled source for conferring authority on individuals and brands. The bar for attaining an entry in Wikipedia is high, but it can be met most easily by securing media coverage.

Wikipedia relies on media coverage to determine which brands meet its "notability" criterion. Candidates for Wikipedia entries must show an extensive trail of citations from reliable sources to clear this bar.

Third-Party Validation Matters More than Ever

While the world of public relations is constantly evolving, there's still no substitute for the third-party validation an earned media story brings to a brand. Not only is it an important tool in building awareness, trust, and credibility within your target market, it's a prerequisite for brands seeking validation from the Big Five websites: Google, Facebook, YouTube, Twitter, and Wikipedia.

When it comes to building trust with target audiences today, earned media coverage from recognized and respected outlets remains one of the surest paths to success.

Strategy #2: Influencer Marketing

Today, celebrity and influencer marketing is all about choosing the right partners—but it hasn't always been that way.

In the late nineties, when I ran PR for a billion-dollar wireless communications company, Burson-Marsteller pitched that we use morning TV weatherman Al Roker as the celebrity spokesman for our latest product launch. They even showed us a video of Roker fumbling awkwardly with the device to illustrate what a great idea it was.

We said no—wisely, I think—to Al. He was famous and a nice guy but had no real connection or expertise that was relevant to us. That was the dimension that was missing.

Of course, that dimension often has been absent in celebrity endorsements. Sheer star power has frequently trumped sensible pairings of endorser and brand.

One of the more infamous examples was when Winston cigarettes sponsored *The Flintstones* and hired Fred Flintstone himself as its celebrity mouthpiece.

"I never smoke nuthin' else," the cartoon caveman proclaimed to a TV audience of children and adults alike.

Influence Has Become More Fragmented—but Also More Relevant

Things have changed over the past fifteen years, since social media came onto the scene.

We still have star-driven campaigns like Matthew McConaughey's iconic ads for Lincoln. But we've also seen an historic extension of the celebrity endorsement from Hollywood stars and professional athletes to tens of thousands of online influencers across Instagram, YouTube, Facebook, TikTok, and other social channels.

With rare exceptions, endorsements are a much more fragmented commodity today. As with virtually all institutions in our society, celebrity is no longer a monolithic status symbol. One person's celebrity is another person's "who?"

Most online influencers can be thought of as *micro-celebrities*, in that few people outside their immediate sphere of influence have ever heard of them. Some niche influencers don't think of themselves as influencers at all—but have followings that can make them valuable avenues for delivering brand messages.

Back when my blog Media Orchard was in its heyday, the pseudonymous blogger known as Strumpette, popularized by Howard Kurtz in *The Washington Post*, dismissed me as a "micro-celebrity." Of course, because I had no ambition to be a celebrity at all, I took it as a compliment. Brands sent me products like high-end cameras to try out in hopes I would write about them on my blog—unsolicited and no questions asked.

Influencer marketing has become far more sophisticated since those early days. A return on investment is expected.

Which brings us to the best thing about influencer endorsements, compared to traditional celebrity endorsements. While celebrities mostly win fans because people enjoy watching them in movies, sports, or TV, influencers typically earn their followings in a targeted niche by creating content specifically for that niche. They have expertise or at least genuine interest in the subject.

That means that niche influencers can actually deliver far more bang for the buck than big-name celebrities—if you know your niche and choose your influencers well.

Know Your Continuum of Influence

We introduced the concept of a continuum of influence in Chapter 2. This continuum begins with the individual consumer who leaves feedback about your brand in a Google review or on a product review site. Those reviews have influence on those who see them.

Beyond review sites, some consumers may have influence on their own platforms on social media. Should they choose to say positive things about you on their channels, this elevates them from simply a consumer to an influencer.

The larger and more relevant an influencer's following, the more important their endorsement becomes. As influencers grow in reach, they move up in category: from nano-influencer to micro-influencer to macro-influencer to mega-influencer.

The relationship of brands with influencers can be paid, organic, or something in between. Traditional organic influencers—like industry analysts or journalists—are usually forbidden from accepting compensation. If they mention your brand, it's because they believe it will be of interest to their audience.

Among paid influencers, compensation varies widely. For smaller influencers, being sent a free sample of a product can be sufficient compensation for a post. An A-list celebrity, meanwhile, might command a million-dollar price tag for a single product mention.

Credibility, Engagement, and Ethics

With all the possibilities, what's the best way to get started with an influencer marketing program that works?

First things first: don't worry about whether the influencer is paid or organic. Even if the influencer is organic, gaining their endorsement costs money—the time and attention you put into finding them and pitching them your story. Focus on whether an influencer has credibility with their audience, and how well that audience matches yours.

Today's top influencers—those with one million or more followers—are closer to reality TV stars than they are to average consumers, which can make them not as influential as you might think. Engagement rates also tend to decline as people's follower counts increase.

Whether working with a nano-influencer or a mega-influencer, a good rule of thumb is to work with influencers who have an average engagement rate of at least 1 percent. But these stats don't tell the whole story, which is why you should carefully review the influencer's content for quality, consistency, and alignment with your brand's messaging and goals.

It's also important to align on the issue of ethics.

Many influencers fall in a gray area between celebrity entertainers and the news media in the minds of their audiences. This can lead to confusion about whether an influencer is offering an honest opinion or simply a paid ad in their endorsements.

Look at an example like *Keeping Up with the Kardashians* star Scott Disick, who has posted paid endorsements not only without writing them, but without reading them either. That's apparently why he inadvertently included his instructions from the advertiser in an Instagram post for the Bootea meal-replacement shake.

The post, under a picture of Disick and a container of the shake, read as follows:

> Here you go, at 4pm est, write the below: 'Keeping up the summer workout routine with my morning @booteauk protein shake!'

Disick made things worse by not including a disclosure that the post was sponsored. A simple three-character hashtag like #ad would have done the trick. Not disclosing sponsored posts actually violates guidelines of the Federal Trade Commission, making the faux pas even more dangerous.

Separating the Real from the Fake

When considering paying an influencer, be sure to check for the following:

- **The influencer clearly discloses partnerships.** If it seems like the influencer is endorsing products and services *without* labeling posts as sponsored, stay away. An influencer unaware of FTC rules—or worse, willing to flout them—is not a trustworthy marketing partner.
- **The influencer's engagement appears legit.** As HBO's 2021 documentary *Fake Famous* illustrates, it's surprisingly easy to fabricate influencer status by buying bots— bots to follow your Instagram account, engage with your posts, buy your book, or even bid for your products on eBay. Idea Grove's social media software partner, Sprout Social, advises any brand considering an

influencer investment to first carefully assess follower-to-engagement rate, engagement quality, sudden spikes in follower count, and audience quality. If something smells fishy, it probably is.

- **The influencer doesn't have reputation issues.** Brands engage with influencers because they want to benefit from their reputation and credibility. If an influencer has received bad press or gets more attention for their controversies than their content, you might want to look elsewhere. Influencers should always reflect the values of your brand.

Using Influencer Endorsements as Website Trust Signals

After you've invested the time and money to attract celebrity and influencer endorsements, it's important to leverage those endorsements wherever possible. That means not only relying on the influencer's social media feed as an inbound trust signal but sharing their seal of approval on your website as well.

Whenever possible, include your top influencers' photos and endorsement quotes on your site, or feature a video in which they describe their experience with your product or service in detail. Even in the case of a paid relationship, audiences can see the difference between someone who actually knows and likes your brand and a Scott Disick who is cutting and pasting endorsements without reading them first.

Influencers and ROI

The best influencer partnerships can yield both short-term and long-term benefits.

For short-term ROI, you should look to the engagement rates on the influencer's posts that mention your brand. Are their followers liking the post? Are they asking questions or seeking to learn more about your product? Can you track sales to the endorsement—and if so, how many? These are all tangible signs of return on investment.

But the even greater return can be as a trust signal for your brand. When you make a celebrity or influencer the face of your brand, the association tends to linger in the memory, particularly for influencers that maintain their visibility over time. That's all the more reason to choose your partners wisely.

Strategy #3: Online Reviews

Let me start this section by acknowledging something we all know, but none of us like.

Life isn't fair.

And as many marketers and business owners have found, online reviews aren't always fair, either.

Let's look at a few unfortunate facts:

- Online reviews do not always represent an accurate sample of customers; for example, people who return products represent a small percentage of buyers but a much larger portion of reviewers.
- Bad reviews have far more influence on buyers than good reviews, with four out of five shoppers specifically seeking out negative reviews and half of those declining to make purchases because of these reviews.
- As many as one in fifteen negative reviews are from people who have never actually purchased the product they

are reviewing but consider themselves "self-appointed brand managers" who want to offer feedback to the seller.

- Some vendors pay shady online reputation management firms to counter negative reviews by posting fake five-star reviews; more than half of electronics reviews on Amazon, for example, have been accused of being fake.

All these things are true. So it's no wonder that some brands simply want to throw up their hands, focus on their business, and hope their hard work will eventually show up in their reviews on Google, Amazon, or Trustpilot.

But here's a second set of facts to consider:

- Nearly nine out of ten consumers read reviews before making a purchase.
- Three in four shoppers say they trust online reviews as much as recommendations from friends, family, and colleagues.
- Google ranks the websites of well-reviewed businesses higher in search results.
- On ecommerce sites, product pages with customer reviews experience 3.5 times more conversions than those without.

Burying your head in the sand when it comes to customer reviews is simply no longer an option. Online reviews rank among the most powerful trust signals for your potential customers, and their influence is only expected to increase in the years ahead.

That's why virtually every brand should implement an aggressive strategy for soliciting and responding to customer reviews.

WHEN SOLICITING ONLINE REVIEWS, AVOID REVIEW GATING

What is *review gating* and why should you care about it?

Review gating is when a business attempts to first find out if a customer's experience was positive or negative before asking for a review—and then only asks for reviews from happy customers. While it might seem like common sense to encourage only your fans to leave online reviews, review gating brings up ethical and legal issues that can put you at odds with Google—and the Federal Trade Commission as well.

In 2019, Google updated its terms of service to discourage review gating in Google Reviews. The terms now say: "Don't discourage or prohibit negative reviews or selectively solicit positive reviews from customers." Other review sites, as well as review management tools such as Birdeye and Podium, quickly issued statements in support of Google's position.

In January 2022, the FTC announced that online retailer Fashion Nova had agreed to pay a $4.2 million fine for concealing bad reviews. The case marked the first time the FTC has stepped in to punish a brand for review gating.

The FTC also sent a letter to ten review management vendors, including Reputation, Signpost, and Grade Us, warning them to avoid the practice.

Ungated Reviews Offer Plenty of Upside, Little Downside

Birdeye, among others, changed its method of soliciting reviews on behalf of their customers after Google's policy change. Whereas before businesses could "pre-check customer sentiment in their review requests," Birdeye updated its interface to solicit reviews from *all* customers after they interacted with a local business—like a restaurant, hair salon, car repair shop, or doctor's office.

What has been the impact of the change? It hasn't been as rough for businesses as you might expect, for a few reasons:

- Customers are much more likely to leave positive than negative reviews when a business directly solicits a review; negative reviews are generally unsolicited.
- Potential customers looking to review sites for guidance can become suspicious when they only see five-star reviews; it's actually better to have a ratio of 5:1 in positive to negative reviews than to have no negative reviews at all.
- If you're able to win over a client who initially had a negative perception of your brand or product, it's even more compelling for prospective buyers.

The review-capturing tool GatherUp, in fact, conducted a study and concluded that not gating reviews leads to more reviews but not significantly lower average star ratings (Blumenthal 2019).

GatherUp sought to answer the question, "Does review gating impact star ratings?" It looked at "roughly 10,000 locations that were in [their] system the year before the switch with gating turned on and compared those same locations after gating was turned off." It found that "gating had very little impact on the average star-rating but that NOT gating saw a significant increase in review volumes."

In the period following the elimination of gating, GatherUp saw review counts grow significantly in the aggregate, by almost 70 percent. Overall ratings on Google and Facebook went down slightly, but almost unnoticeably.

On Google, for example, average star ratings declined from 4.66 to 4.59 without any filtering or selective solicitation. However, review volumes grew from over 32,000 to more than 53,000 on Google.

Since review volume is a trust signal that a product or service is popular, the upside of ungating reviews clearly outweighs the downside risk.

It also keeps you out of trouble with Google and the FTC.

How to Create a Review Presence That Grows Trust

No matter your industry or profession, it's much easier for your business to grow sales if you first implement a review strategy that grows trust.

Here are five steps to creating or enhancing your online-review strategy:

#1: Address Any Product or Operational Issues
Driving Negative Reviews

There's no point in putting time and effort into a review program if you don't first address the chronic issues that reviewers complain about. Study reviews carefully to identify common themes and address complaints. It's critical to get your house in order before inviting people to visit.

#2: Determine Which Review Sites Should Be Your Priorities

Review sites have become a big business, with hundreds of sites competing for attention. It's important to focus your efforts on the three to five sites that are most important to your business. Virtually every brand should care about Google, which accounts for more than half of all online reviews. The rest will depend on your type of business.

#3: Create a System for Asking Your Customers for Reviews

What's the best way to ask for reviews? Local service businesses, like restaurants, hotels, and hair salons, should take the direct route by asking the customer for a review before they ever leave your place of business. For pure ecommerce companies, follow up with your customer right after their purchase with an email or text message that links to the site where you'd like their review to appear. For companies that sell products or services that require some time to evaluate, set up a quarterly Net Promoter Score (NPS) survey and ask for reviews at that time.

#4: Embed Positive Reviews on Your Website

Many review sites enable you to embed reviews directly from their site onto yours. Where to embed reviews? If you have individual products that are reviewed, embed those reviews on the relevant product pages within your site. If the reviews speak to your company as a whole, add them to your home page. And for online merchants, embedded reviews in the checkout process have been shown to increase conversions.

#5: Respond to All Reviews, Whether Negative, Positive, or Mixed

While some business owners think they should only respond to negative reviews, it's a good idea to respond to all reviews. Always respond sincerely, acknowledge the reviewer's specific situation, and never argue or act defensive. We'll discuss responding to negative reviews and social media complaints more in Chapter 12.

With an equal focus on the news media, social media influencers, and customer reviews, a third-party validation strategy can build a pathway of trust to your website—and ultimately to growth.

CHAPTER 12

Playing Defense— Reputation Management

→ The best defense for your brand's reputation is a good offense; establish a positive presence in the news media, on social media, and on review sites.

→ Adopt a social purpose to give your reputation management strategy clarity and context—but don't fake it.

→ In today's twenty-four-hour information cycle, respond to complaints, crises, and conspiracy theories with urgency, humility, and tact.

To borrow a phrase from George W. Bush's now-famous critique of President Trump's 2017 inaugural address: people are believing some "weird shit" these days.

Such as the following:

Starting on the social media site Reddit and spreading like wildfire across the internet, thousands of people shared content in July 2021 accusing the furniture retailer Wayfair of trafficking children. These charges were not based on police investigations, journalistic reporting, or firsthand accounts.

What evidence was there to support these allegations? None.

The original post on Reddit was pure speculation after the poster found utility closets on the Wayfair site priced at more than $10,000 each—with girls' names as product names.

The post read:

> Is it possible Wayfair involved in Human Trafficking? Or are these just extremely overpriced cabinets? This makes me sick to my stomach if it's true.

That was on July 9. By the next day, Wayfair was compelled to issue a statement that "there is, of course, no truth to these claims." *Snopes* and other sources verified that the rumor was false.

But even now, hashtags like #wayfairtrafficking are active on social media.

In our post-truth world, social media algorithms too often reward behavior that promotes controversy and misinformation. Those who lead cancel-culture crusades and spread conspiracy theories, for example, earn the "social currency" of status and popularity—while rarely being held to account for their damaging claims legally or financially.

That makes this an especially challenging environment for reputation management.

WHAT IS REPUTATION MANAGEMENT?

Reputation has always mattered. We might not have had to worry about cancel culture or bad online reviews in the past, but there's never been a time when people didn't gossip with their friends and neighbors about other people.

Consumers today talk about businesses the same way—backed by a social-media megaphone that can make or break a brand.

Think of reputation management as PR playing defense, such as when:

- your customers are posting one-star Google reviews,
- your employees are trashing you on Glassdoor,
- a lawsuit against your company appears high in your branded search results,
- a negative news story accuses you of incompetence or misdeeds, or
- you or one of your employees gets "canceled" on Twitter for a bad decision or a poor choice of words.

Over the past three decades, I have managed crises ranging from massive telecom outages to workplace shootings and sex scandals.

And while the environment has grown more challenging, one thing that hasn't changed is this: the best defense is a good offense. The sturdier the reputation you build over time, the better equipped you will be to protect it in critical moments.

REPUTATION MANAGEMENT STRATEGIES TO BUILD AND PROTECT TRUST

Within the Grow With TRUST system, reputation management is arguably the most critical component—because what's the point in working so hard to build your brand only to risk losing it all in an instant?

The three key pillars of reputation management are as follows:

1. **Proactive reputation building.** Establish a positive presence in the news media, social media, and review sites—then consider making it stronger with social purpose.
2. **Crisis preparation strategy.** Start by tackling your current operational issues. Then, anticipate future issues before they occur.
3. **Monitoring and response strategy.** People won't wait long for a reply to their complaint. Respond with urgency, humility, and tact.

Pursuing a Grow With TRUST program without strong reputation management is like setting off on a cross-country car ride without fastening your seatbelt. You might make it, but it's not worth the risk.

Strategy #1: Proactive Reputation Building

One Saturday night years ago, I went to a party at a coworker's house and a woman there got very drunk. She was a new employee at the newspaper where I worked and was probably nervous. She responded by going too heavy on the liquid courage.

The highlight—or lowlight—of the evening was when she mistook the laundry room for the bathroom and tried to relieve herself in the dryer.

She didn't show up for work that Monday. We never saw her again.

This is someone who did not manage her reputation well and suffered the consequences.

But let's imagine the scenario differently. What if, instead of this being a new employee, it had been a reporter who had worked at the paper for ten years? What if she had a reputation for being a hard-working, responsible, and caring person, and this was the first time she had ever had too much to drink in the presence of her colleagues?

That reporter would have shown up for work Monday and been welcomed back with open arms. She would have probably had to take some good-natured ribbing. Maybe her editor might show some concern and ask if things were OK in her personal life. But that would be the end of it; everybody would move on.

That's the difference between a person we know and respect making a mistake, and someone we don't.

And it's the same way for brands.

Channels for Building Your Brand Reputation

Third-party validation and reputation management go hand in hand. Your reputation is much easier to defend if you have established a positive image and strong relationships in the news media, social media, and review sites.

These are the three primary channels for proactive reputation management. They can help preserve your reputation when the time comes. Here's how:

News Media

You never want your first contact with the news media to be during a crisis when you are on the defensive. Work to establish media relationships that will humanize your executives and provide a broader context for your brand.

Also, make sure that when a reporter searches for your brand on Google, they will find lots of positive information to build trust, such as five-star reviews and happy team photos. It will balance their view of your brand.

Social Media

Many brands—particularly B2B brands—complain that they see little ROI from social media. But social media is not primarily a sales platform; it's a relationship platform. You are establishing your foothold on a site trusted by millions or, in some cases, hundreds of millions of users.

Having an active presence on LinkedIn, Twitter, Facebook, and other top sites allows you to share your values, comment on the topics of the day, and amplify your thought leadership. It also gives you a solid foundation for interacting with customers and responding to complaints and crises.

Online Reviews

Top review sites include Google, Yelp, Facebook, and BBB.org, but beyond those, literally thousands of review sites have emerged for specific niches and industries. Establish a presence on the sites that are most important to your brand, create detailed profiles with images and product descriptions, and then, invite your customers to leave reviews after a transaction or during a follow-up later. This provides context and balance when an unhappy customer leaves a negative review.

Establishing a positive brand presence in these channels is the best proactive step you can take to protect yourself when challenges come. You may also consider another step that will strengthen and provide content for these channels: *adopting a social purpose.*

Social Purpose: Give Your Brand a Higher Meaning

As we discussed in Chapter 9, buyers today care about more than your product. When buyers make purchase decisions, they often factor in whether the brand is one they wish to align with—based on the brand's social and political stances and other considerations.

Over the past few years, surveys have consistently shown that more consumers are factoring a company's values into their buying decisions. Two-thirds of consumers around the world will buy or boycott a brand solely because of its position on a social or political issue, according to the global PR firm Edelman's research.

Avoiding social issues entirely is viewed negatively by consumers —as a sign that a brand doesn't care.

And it's not just buyers; it's employees, too. Job seekers increasingly seek to work for employers that stand for something besides profits.

How should a brand navigate these new expectations?

You have three choices.

1. You can stick to selling your product and stay out of social and political issues altogether.
2. You can create a Corporate Social Responsibility (CSR) program, contributing to your community in ways that are ancillary to your business, such as building Habitat for Humanity houses on the weekends.
3. You can adopt a social purpose—transforming your brand into one whose entire reason for being is to build a better world.

Brands have every right to choose the first or second option. Consumers, however, are increasingly pushing their favorite brands in the direction of social purpose.

Adopting a social purpose means fusing your company's product offering with a larger vision for making the world a better place. Embracing purpose helps to unify your audiences, giving your brand an edge over those who appear to only care about the bottom line.

In a 2021 survey of one thousand US adults by PR firm Porter Novelli, 73 percent said they were less likely to "cancel" a purpose-driven brand ("Business of Cancel Culture Study").

Social purpose can also give your reputation management strategy clarity and context.

Specifically:

- It provides evidence of your commitment to issues your customers care about.
- It aligns purchases of your product with making the world a better place.
- It provides a steady stream of positive content for social media and potential news coverage.

But social purpose is not like a traditional CSR program:

- CSR programs are often little more than feel-good sidelights to your brand.
- A social purpose is core to your brand. In many ways, it defines your brand.
- Audiences can tell if you are faking it. If your heart isn't in it or your words aren't backed by action, your efforts will ultimately damage brand trust.

If you are not ready to embrace a larger "why" for what you do, you're not ready for social purpose.

PURPOSE CAN BE PROFITABLE

For both B2C and B2B brands, purpose can be profitable.

Danish toymaker LEGO is an $8 billion company that generated nearly $2 billion in profit in 2021—a 27 percent increase in revenue over the year before (Whitten 2022; Tighe 2022).

LEGO has long associated its products with helping children learn and grow—to "inspire and develop the builders of tomorrow."

LEGO extends this brand promise to a larger social purpose. The brand has consistently invested in initiatives to enrich, nurture, and protect the future of children. These include:

- sustainability initiatives,
- online safety for children, and
- DEI programs.

Not coincidentally, LEGO ranked as the "most reputable company in the world" in RepTrak's 2021 annual survey for the second year in a row (LEGO Group).

But purpose isn't just for B2C products like children's toys. It can give B2B brands a competitive edge as well.

While some B2B brands have begun viewing social purpose as important to growth, many are unsure how to embed their stated purpose into every aspect of their operations. To build brand trust, both with customers and with employees, your brand purpose must be relevant to your company and customer base.

As an example, in 2018 Dropbox and its founders launched the Dropbox Foundation, which focuses on partnering with nonprofits to promote human rights. As a service that enables millions of users to easily share information, Dropbox's support for organizations that use information to defend human rights fits their brand.

As the company put it: "A big part of our mission has always been helping our users achieve *their* missions."

Four Advantages
for Purpose-Driven B2Bs

The advantages for B2Bs adopting a social purpose include:

#1: Differentiating Your Brand Based on Values

There were more than 1,000 initial public offerings on the US stock market in 2021, an all-time record. That was more than double the 480 IPOs the year before—also a record. In a crowded marketplace, having a clearly stated purpose and actions to support it can help differentiate your brand by appealing to buyers' emotions and values.

#2: Aligning with Your Buyer's Vendor Selection Criteria

B2B buyers are increasingly responsible for upholding their own companies' social responsibility initiatives, such as sustainability and DEI. Choosing vendors aligned on these issues is increasingly important to them—and in some cases a mandate.

#3: Making the Purchase Decision Easier

The B2B buying process can take months, even years, involving stakeholders at various levels of the organization. Building strong brand identification and trust with buyers can reduce these sales cycles. Microsoft, for example, makes an even stronger case for its products and services by elevating its CSR programs, such as committing to being carbon negative by 2030.

> **#4: Attracting Purpose-Driven Candidates to the Company**
>
> Today's workforce increasingly wants to feel connected with the purpose and mission of the companies they work for. Employees want to know they are contributing to the world in some way. Companies with social purpose built into their culture are more likely to attract and retain an engaged workforce.

Strategy #2: Crisis Preparation

When it comes to crisis preparation and planning, the first thing to understand is that you can't erase reality.

Or as a reputation management consultant I know once put it: "If you suck in real life, you'll suck on the internet."

The first step in preparing for a crisis is to take a hard look at yourself—from the viewpoints of others. Use sentiment analysis tools to see what people are saying about you on social media. Read your online reviews with an open mind to find the common threads in customer complaints. Conduct interviews with customers and survey your target audiences to see what they think of your brand.

Correct the issues that surface. They won't go away by themselves.

There's no point in putting time and effort into responding to online complaints if you don't first address the operational issues driving them. Amazingly, nearly a third of local businesses admit in surveys they *don't read their reviews at all*. That's a wasted opportunity to get better.

When you do make improvements to your business, make sure to let your audiences know about it across your marketing channels—and thank your critics for their feedback. They will be flattered, and more likely to purchase from you again, too.

Failing to Anticipate Is Often the Biggest Mistake

If your brand has made mistakes in the past, it's likely you will make them in the future, too. We all do, after all.

The key is to catch as many of those potential missteps as possible while they are still being kicked around internally. Run them through the filter of your audience research. When you know what your customers value and expect from your brand, you should be able to stop most crises before they start.

Take Swedish vegan milk brand Oatly, long a favorite of eco-friendly consumers. In 2020, private equity firm Blackstone—led by CEO Stephen Schwarzman, who had served in the Trump administration—spearheaded a $200 million funding round for the company. The company justified the investment in a July 2020 announcement as channeling "more capital flows into sustainability" from across the political spectrum.

Oatly should have expected its customer base to have issues with Blackstone, given President Trump's views on climate change and other environmental issues. Unfortunately, Oatly made little effort to educate and win over eco-influencers, even weeks after the announcement.

Predictably, by the end of August, these influencers had mobilized a boycott. It kicked off with a tweet by @LessWasteLaura, a climate activist who had just learned of Blackstone's investment. Many customers responded as if Oatly had cut a secret deal behind their backs—even though it had been publicly announced more than a month prior.

Oatly had an opportunity to raise awareness and make their case to activists before the controversy became a cancellation effort. Instead, they lost control of the narrative, leading to the loss of some of the brand's most vocal ambassadors.

The shedding of core fans has left the company vulnerable to a torrent of negative stories and business setbacks. Oatly has been accused of "greenwashing," or misleading consumers about its sustainability practices, as well as overstating revenues and other forms of deception. Its former activist base has been nowhere to be found.

HOW TO FIGHT CONSPIRACY THEORIES

Conspiracy theories are more frequent, more widespread, and less easily contained than ever before—as we described, at the outset of this chapter, in documenting the false allegations against Wayfair.

So, if your brand comes under attack, as Wayfair's did, what's the best way to fight back? Here are three tips based on my years in crisis communications and reputation management.

#1: Calibrate Your Denial Carefully

As most brands would, Wayfair quickly and flatly denied any truth to the rumor. This is a necessary action, but it's just as important not to make too big a deal out of it. If you shout denials from the rooftops—correcting every false post, issuing multiple press releases, etc.—it will hurt more than help you.

Overdoing it will also further cement your brand's association with the conspiracy theory, as well as alert users who were previously unaware of the rumor.

#2: Deprive the Rumors of Oxygen with Positive Messages

Conspiracy theories don't stand up to rational analysis, so a reasoned denial will only take you so far. A more sustainable strategy is to *counterprogram* by investing in PR campaigns that share the positive things your brand is doing in the community.

Where appropriate, you can even fight a negative rumor more directly. For example, if a conspiracy theory suggests your brand is anti-Muslim, anti-LGBTQ, or opposed to another group, prominently include members of that group on your website and in community outreach efforts.

Go beyond window dressing with substantive action, such as creating diversity and inclusion programs at your company and donating to nonprofit organizations. That will protect your brand far better in the long run than an endless stream of denials.

#3: Encourage Your Customers to Tell Your Story

Whether denying a false rumor or countering it with positive messages, there's still one problem: it's *you* talking. That's why it's important to encourage your customer advocates to be visible and vocal in support of your brand.

Provide a great product and outstanding customer service so your customers will want to tell everyone about it. Set up programs to periodically nudge your customers to post reviews on Google, Yelp, G2, TrustRadius, or other review sites. There's no better way to build trust with consumers than with third-party validation.

Run a Check on Your Execs to Prevent Surprises

Don't stop with your brand or product when anticipating issues, though. Take a close look at your brand's representatives—your executives and subject-matter experts—as well.

Cancel culture can come for anyone, including your CEO. Look at the example of Condé Nast and its publication *Teen Vogue*. In May 2021, Alexi McCammond, the newly appointed editor-in-chief, was forced to step down because of tweets she had written ten years earlier—when she was seventeen.

Search for anything questionable your execs and spokespeople have posted on social media—ever—and delete it. Do a Google search as well. And, if you haven't already done so, run a background check that confirms professional credentials and reveals any past legal issues. It's worth it.

Don't Use Your Crisis Plan as a Crutch

I'm going to let you in on a little secret: that crisis communications plan every consultant says you should have? It's an important tool for planning—but it's not enough to get you through a crisis. Too often, it's used as a crutch by those fearful of taking bold, decisive action.

Years ago, during a massive satellite outage that affected telecom services for fifty million Americans, I was the face of the crisis for my industry, simply because the other telecom companies affected were slow to release statements and make themselves available to the public. I'm sure all those companies had crisis plans—but they still didn't pick up the phones to field calls from reporters seeking answers.

I honestly can't recall if I looked at our crisis plan during that outage. I was too busy gathering the latest information available and then, every hour on the hour, doing stand-up interviews for local and national TV. My team ensured that the trade media got the more technical information they were seeking, too.

We put ourselves—vulnerable and imperfect—front and center. And that was enough. Our response had a halo effect on our brand that reinforced our claim of being the industry leader.

Get on the Same Page with the Lawyers

In my experience, the most valuable benefit of a crisis plan is that it gets the company's executives, marketers, communicators, and attorneys on the same page on how to approach crises.

I've found that without a clear plan, PR people and corporate attorneys usually end up butting heads.

Attorneys tend to focus first on reducing legal risk, which is important—but this approach can increase reputation risk if taken too far. For example, responding to a crisis with "No comment" may be the safest option legally, but it's the ultimate PR mistake.

When Exxon failed to send its CEO immediately to the scene of the infamous Valdez oil spill, it was evident that lawyers, not PR people, were behind the decision. The episode is widely considered one of the greatest PR blunders of all time.

Strategy #3: Monitoring and Response

Many people are unaware that the modern public relations industry grew out of a reputation management crisis. On October 28, 1906, a Pennsylvania Railroad train crashed, killing more than fifty passengers. The railroad called on one of PR's founding fathers, Ivy Lee, to help (News Museum, n.d.).

Lee might not have had the vision of Edward Bernays, but he was among the first PR practitioners to convince big corporations to come clean when they made mistakes.

Before Lee, US railroads mostly downplayed accidents, sometimes refusing to admit they occurred. They hid evidence and kept journalists away from crash sites. Lee changed all that by actually inviting reporters to the scene, holding on-site briefings, and making executives available for interviews.

The result was what scholars characterized as the first positive news coverage for the railroad industry in years.

Lee worked with speed and transparency to respond to reporters and protect the railroad's reputation. That's the same way it works today—except that events move exponentially faster, and the audience isn't just the media, but anyone with access to social media.

Responding to Customers on Online Review Sites

If it hasn't already happened to your business, it surely will at some point: an unhappy customer will post a negative review, and your prospective customers will read it.

The good news is that those same prospects will think better of you if you leave a response to that review. In fact, nearly half of those surveyed by the reputation management software company ReviewTrackers (2021) said they were more likely to visit businesses that responded to bad reviews.

In other words, there's plenty of upside, and virtually no downside, to responding to online reviews. This includes not only negative reviews but also positive ones. Prospects are more likely to read reviews with a company response. That means if you respond to a positive review, it serves to reinforce that review and draw more attention to it.

Your responses are an opportunity to make amends with unsatisfied customers, thank happy customers—and build trust with prospects.

No matter what kind of review you've received, there are several no-nos to always keep in mind:

- Don't respond based on emotion.
- Avoid excuses and justifications.
- Don't blame or argue with the reviewer.
- Never leave a one-line response like "Thank you" or "Sorry for your experience."
- Don't post a response that seems cookie-cutter or insincere.
- Never ignore a negative review.

Finally, try to respond to reviews within twenty-four hours. New reviews are generally what review site visitors see first, so you want them to see your response as well.

Responding quickly also makes it more likely the reviewer will see your response—which can help reinforce a positive customer experience or defuse a negative one.

DON'T LET YOUR REPUTATION MANAGEMENT
AGENCY RUIN YOUR REPUTATION

We live our lives online today. Hence, how we appear in a Google search is more important than a mention in a newspaper article. That's why PR today must take a broader approach to building and maintaining reputation—one encompassing all the ways audiences gain or lose trust in brands.

Traditional PR practitioners, unfortunately, were slow to adapt to the online world, creating an opportunity for digital marketers to hang up shingles proclaiming their expertise in "online reputation management," or ORM. An entirely new cottage industry emerged, beginning with the launch of companies like Reputation-Defender in 2006.

While traditional PR practitioners still focused on press releases and media outreach, ORM began operating behind the scenes to improve Google search results for their clients. This included activities to "push down" or even remove negative search results—such as bad online reviews and news stories.

The Risks of Black-Hat ORM

While some ORM practitioners have high ethical standards (ReputationDefender, now owned by NortonLifeLock, is one of them), many others do not. Similar to black-hat SEO firms, these firms offer a quick fix rather than getting to the root of a reputation problem. They work in a manner inconsistent with PRSA's Code of Ethics—and are therefore risky for their clients' reputations.

Some of the questionable practices of ORM firms include the following:

- Creating fake reviews to try to push down negative reviews and increase a client's star rating on review sites
- Buying backlinks in violation of Google's policies to artificially improve the search position of positive content
- Buying mentions with under-the-table payments in articles on popular publications and blogs
- Creating Wikipedia pages for clients against Wikipedia's guidelines
- Posting knowingly false information, such as claiming a client has given to charities or won awards when it hasn't

The Ethical Alternative

As ethical PR firms get up to speed on ORM, many are bringing a different mindset to online reputation—one that takes the longer view. The right way to improve a reputation includes the following:

- Consulting with the client to get at the core of reputational issues
- Developing a plan to communicate actual changes in the business to address these issues
- Responding to unhappy customers on social media and review sites and making amends
- Identifying happy customers through Net Promoter Score (NPS) surveys and encouraging them to leave authentic positive reviews

- Earning positive media coverage to tell the client's side of the story and show the client has overcome its reputational issues

Choosing the Right Agency Partner

Taking a more strategic (and ethical) view of ORM doesn't mean you can't address issues quickly.

At Idea Grove, we had a client—a global midmarket company with a long-standing positive reputation—that had been acquired two years earlier. Rapid changes in leadership, organizational structure, and product strategy led to dozens of negative Glassdoor reviews—a turnoff to prospective employees and clients alike.

Even with swift changes to improve employee morale and an active internal NPS program, it can take months to improve a poor Glassdoor rating. The client wanted the public to know about its positive internal changes sooner than that.

So we recommended that they set up authentic profiles, with authentic reviews, on alternative employer review sites. These sites are not as well known as Glassdoor, but by establishing a presence on them, the client could draw those reviews to the first page of its branded search results to enhance its reputation.

Reputation management will continue to change. When selecting an agency to help navigate this landscape, choose one that adheres to ethical standards of conduct, such as PRSA's Code of Ethics. It's the right thing to do and will achieve more lasting results over time.

Responding to Negative Comments on Social Media

While a twenty-four-hour response time works for online review sites, the rules are different on social media sites like Facebook and Twitter.

Your response time must be even faster.

Research by Sprout Social shows that even though 63 percent of social media complaints receive replies within twenty-four hours, most consumers are not happy with that response time. Nearly 40 percent expect a response within *an hour* of posting their complaint ("Social Media Trends for 2022 & Beyond").

If you think about it, it makes sense. Many consumers turn to Facebook or Twitter to complain only after going through the brand's usual channels and having a frustrating experience.

By the time they vent on social media, they have run out of patience. Have empathy for them.

To catch and respond to social media complaints quickly, make sure to use a tool for real-time social listening and brand monitoring. (Sprout Social, an Idea Grove partner, is a good one.) This will allow you to track mentions of your brand, executives, and competitors as they happen—as well as red flags like spikes in activity and negative sentiment.

Winning with Urgency, Humility, and Tact

Particularly for popular and high-profile brands, reputation management is hard work. But it's worth it.

The surest way to survive and succeed in a post-truth world of crises, cancellations, and conspiracies is with trust. Choose a set of values and stick to them. Hope for the best but prepare for the worst.

Remember, people are believing some "weird shit" these days, so show urgency, humility, and tact when communicating with your customers—because your brand wouldn't exist without them.

CHAPTER 13

Making Connections— User Experience

→ Building a brand isn't about cool logos and pricey ad campaigns; it's about projecting a consistent face for your business.

→ Design a trust-centered website that focuses less on visual pyrotechnics and more on making visitors feel at home.

→ Use empathy and relevance to grow trust at every stage of the buying cycle, from your website to your marketing emails.

J eff Bezos once famously said, "A brand for a company is like a reputation for a person."

I'll take that wisdom a step further. The true test of a brand is whether its customers *treat it like a person*. Branding, after all, is about conferring human traits on things that aren't human in order to build trust—and to use that trust to create value.

Think about it: every company—even household names like Amazon, Nike, and Disney—is ultimately nothing more than a set of documents filed by a lawyer somewhere. Corporations are legal entities created specifically to keep their activities separate from those of the people who formed them (for liability, tax, and other reasons).

And despite the US Supreme Court granting corporations the rights and protections of "personhood," they are decidedly *not* human (Torres-Spelliscy 2014). Not only that, but the humans who are part of these entities—founders, leaders, employees, shareholders—can come and go as they please. If they all departed at once, all that would be left is the legal filings.

So what is a corporation at its heart?

The answer is up to you as a marketer, entrepreneur, or CEO. Its heart is the heart you give it.

BRANDS EXIST TO PROJECT A CONSISTENT
FACE FOR THE BUSINESS

Given the fact that every person who is part of a business can leave it at any time, it makes sense that Job 1 for any brand is to communicate continuity. Branding is not a marketing gimmick; it's the glue that holds companies together.

Whenever a shareholder sells their stock in a company, the buyer has certain expectations of continuity. The company's leadership is expected to meet these expectations—not only in terms of financial performance, but by having a predictable business model that shareholders can count on for the long term.

That's where branding comes in. Branding communicates the enduring qualities of a company's business model.

It says, *"This is the kind of person we are—if we were actually a person."*

So Disney is family-oriented, fun, and magical. Nike is active, bold, and inspirational. And so on.

To the extent a company's logo, colors, products, advertising, and other projections of itself support these traits, the brand builds continuity—which, over time, can become a company's most valuable asset.

Brands further humanize themselves by engaging with the world beyond their product. This includes embracing social purpose, which we discussed in the last chapter, and thought leadership, which we will discuss in Chapter 15. You might think of social purpose and thought leadership as the heart and head of your brand.

Unfortunately, cool logos and big ad campaigns are what too many marketers and business leaders focus on in their branding efforts. They would do well to remember the ultimate reason their brand exists in the first place: to project a consistent face for the business.

EMBEDDING YOUR BRAND IN THE USER EXPERIENCE

That's what makes user experience so important to building trust. Brands must be *ruthlessly consistent* in how they present themselves across *multiple* channels and touchpoints. That's challenging but crucial—because if you're inconsistent, your audiences won't be sure of who you really are.

Think of it this way. When you first meet a person, you start to develop ideas about them based on your interactions. If they act differently toward you from one day to the next, you eventually begin to distrust them. You're not sure exactly who you're dealing with.

It's the same way with brands. If your website copy is formal and detached but your email marketing is casual and intimate, your buyers begin to wonder about you. Brand inconsistency leads to mixed signals and, ultimately, mistrust.

That's why user experience should start with your website but must then extend to all of your brand's owned media, defined as anything under the brand's direct control, such as your blog, emails, social media channels, and sell sheets. Your brand must also establish relevance with your customers at each stage of the buyer's journey.

USER EXPERIENCE STRATEGIES TO BUILD CONNECTION AND TRUST

We listed twenty-nine website trust signals in Chapters 4 and 5, ranging from third-party trust seals to professional design and quality content. Extending the scope of user experience to all owned media, the three key pillars of user experience strategy are as follows:

1. **Trust-centered website design.** Your website is your home online; make it feel like home for your visitors, too.
2. **Owned media strategy.** Establish a message and voice that is consistent across every vehicle you own or control.

3. **Full-funnel content strategy.** The keys to building trust at every stage of the marketing funnel are empathy and relevance.

By repeating the same messaging, tone, and visual identity across all owned media, a consistent user experience increases brand recall, while building the trust that comes with a steady brand voice.

If you've done your research, this voice will resonate with your buyers and other audiences.

TRUE-BLUE TRUST:

BRAND COLORS AND USER EXPERIENCE

Have you ever noticed how many brands use the color blue in their logos and on their websites?

The reason is simple: they want you to *trust* them.

Blue is the single most frequently used color in corporate logos. It's especially common in brands where trust is paramount, such as financial services, cybersecurity, and healthcare.

Why the connection between blue and trust?

The most common theory is that we typically have positive associations with blue—and from the sky to the sea, these associations evoke feelings of security and permanence. Research has consistently shown blue to be the favorite color of both men and women worldwide.

Etymologically, the term "true blue" has been used to describe trustworthiness for centuries. In the Late Medieval Period, the town of Coventry, England, was known for its talented dyers. Dyeing clothing and fabrics in those days—using sometimes poisonous berries and plants to create pigment—was a job that was both tedious and dangerous. The dyers of Coventry were renowned for producing blue cloth that could be trusted to never fade.

The phrase "as true as Coventry blue" was shortened to "true blue" and the rest is history.

Don't Be Blue: It's OK to Be a Different Color, Too

With trust being so important to buyers, and buyers associating trust with the color blue, does that mean it's always preferable to include blue in your brand's logo?

Definitely not.

First and foremost, your company's branding should help set you apart from the competition. If every competitor in your space has a blue logo, having blue as the dominant color in your logo will make it that much harder for you to stand out.

At Idea Grove, we work with many midsize B2B tech brands in highly competitive markets where our clients must fight tooth and nail for their share of attention—and customers—while facing much larger players.

We recently completed a visual branding project in which the logo we created had purple and black as its dominant colors. Based on color theory, the purple communicates imagination and luxury, while the black grounds the logo in authority. This combination was perfect for a brand that wanted to communicate creativity while being taken seriously by its Fortune 500 clients.

The client's logo inspires trust *by reinforcing the qualities that set it apart.* It's a subconscious trust signal that the company backs up its words with its actions.

Trust signals like color might be subconscious, but they are trust signals nonetheless. Be sure to align them with your brand.

Strategy #1: Trust-Centered Website Design

If you've ever solicited bids for a website project, you've no doubt had agencies come and present to you. You might have noticed the majority of the pitches fall into one of two camps.

Some firms try to wow you with visually acrobatic designs that have an appeal similar to a fireworks display.

Boom. Bang. Pop.

Other agencies talk about transactional lead generation. They seem to think telling your company's story is a simple arithmetic equation.

Input content, output sales.

It doesn't work that way.

The reality is this:

If your visitors don't believe you, nothing else matters.

That means your first priority should be to find an agency that understands audience trust and how to achieve it.

At Idea Grove, we call it *trust-centered web design.*

A trust-centered web design firm takes the time to understand your business, your product, your customers, and your other audiences. It knows the trust signals that make a visitor want to learn more about you. Understanding and applying these trust signals requires knowledge and expertise.

Because without trust, the visual pyrotechnics and lead-gen formulas mean nothing.

Why Your *About Us* Page Is Crucial to Building Trust

One of the website trust signals we referenced in Chapter 5 is the *About Us* page.

For many brands, the *About Us* page is the second most popular destination after the home page. That means your visitors want to know who you are and what you're about—and they may never make it to your product and pricing pages if they don't like what they see.

I advise my agency's clients to approach the task of creating an *About Us* page boldly—like a *superhero origin story*.

Have you ever wondered *why* so many superhero movies are origin stories—focused on that moment when a regular person becomes a superhero? Some argue that audiences love to witness the dramatic change when an ordinary person becomes superhuman. We fantasize about making that transformation ourselves, the theory goes.

I disagree, though. I think their true appeal is best explained by the clinical psychologist Robin Rosenberg (2013). Writing for *Smithsonian Magazine*, she put it this way:

> I think origin stories show us not how to become super but how to be heroes, choosing altruism over the pursuit of wealth and power...At their best, superhero origin stories inspire us and provide models of coping with adversity, finding meaning in loss and trauma, discovering our strengths and using them for good purpose.

And that is the model that every business should use to describe itself to its audiences.

What's Your Superhero Story?

Telling your superhero story begins with the nuts and bolts—the 5Ws:

- *Who* are your company's leaders?
- *What* are your company's mission and goals?
- *When* did you realize you had an idea that could help people?
- *Where* are you better than the other guys?
- *Why* should buyers trust you enough to do business with you?

Most *About Us* pages include some or all of these components. Unfortunately, they are often written as an afterthought and with little narrative flair. That's a huge missed opportunity.

So, are you ready to give your own origin story the superhero treatment? Believe me, you can do it.

To inspire you, here's an example—from the San Francisco-based Yellow Leaf Hammocks:

In 2011, while on vacation in Thailand, our co-founder Joe embarked on an impromptu motorcycle adventure that led him to discover the world's most comfortable hammock hanging outside a hut on a tiny island.

The hammocks were unlike anything Joe had ever seen or felt before, and he knew he had to share them with the world. He bought as many as he could fit in his backpack and headed home, ready to turn his vacation dream into a reality.

Joe teamed up with his now-wife Rachel to establish Yellow Leaf—bringing a curated collection of beautifully crafted, ultra-comfortable hammocks to the masses, while giving back to the original crafters of the world's most comfortable hammocks.

Each individual Yellow Leaf hammock is handwoven with the utmost precision and care by the expert craftswomen of the Mlabri Tribe—"the people of the yellow leaves"—in the hills of Northern Thailand. Across three weaving communities, we are working to create jobs for mothers and build a foundation for positive community transformation.

Doing good while relaxing? We can hang with that.

That's a superhero story. And I believe if you dig deep enough, every brand has one—unique to its own audience, brand message, and voice.

Delivering trust signals like this throughout your website is the essence of trust-centered design.

Strategy #2: Owned Media

While your website should be the center of gravity for your brand's online presence, it shouldn't be your whole world.

Ever since Benjamin Franklin first published *Poor Richard's Almanack* to promote his printing business in 1732, businesses have used a wide variety of owned media, from mail-order catalogs to travel guides to company magazines, to build trust and grow their brands.

Some brands have taken off with blogs, like Moz, which has

become as well-known for SEO news as it has for SEO software, and podcasts, like AARP's *The Perfect Scam*, a true-crime series that dramatically increased the visibility of the nonprofit group's Fraud Watch Network.

And LEGO achieved perhaps the greatest owned-media feat of all—turning out a series of Hollywood blockbusters promoting its little plastic bricks, starting with *The LEGO Movie* in 2014.

Of course, you don't need to go that big. Owned media also includes the monthly newsletter you send to your email list and the tweets and posts you share on social media.

That's why every brand needs an overarching owned-media strategy that accounts for the online assets you control or manage, including the following:

- Your blog
- Your company newsletters
- Your marketing emails
- Your webinars
- Your podcast
- Your explainer video
- Your demo video
- Your YouTube channel
- Your original music
- Your social media posts
- Your sell sheets
- Your sales decks
- Your online magazines
- Your catalogs
- Forums you manage

- Secondary websites or apps
- Live chat and texts

Owned media tends to be a longer-term investment than earned or paid media. It takes time to build a blog readership, podcast audience, email subscriber list, or social media following. So it's important to choose your investments wisely based on audience research and budget priorities.

It's better not to start a podcast at all than to abandon it after a few episodes. That's wasted time and effort.

And it commits the greatest brand sin of all: inconsistency.

Creating Consistency across Owned Media

As we discussed at the outset of this chapter, the first job of branding is not creativity—it's continuity.

So what's the best way to maintain a consistent look, voice, and message across all your owned-media channels—which each might be managed by different in-house staff or external agencies?

The key is to create, set, and communicate brand standards and to make sure they are observed across your organization.

Your brand standards should include both visual design standards and brand messaging guidelines. Brand guides establish rules for logo usage, fonts, colors, and typography, along with the brand's positioning, purpose, and personality.

A brand's message platform should contain the following components:

- **Brand essence**—the core benefit you deliver to buyers
- **Brand voice**—the personality of your brand

- **Brand purpose**—how you make the world a better place
- **Brand positioning**—how you differentiate yourself in the market
- **Elevator pitch**—how you describe yourself to the market
- **Messaging framework**—key taglines, value proposition, and three or more core message statements with proof points

The message platform tells your audiences who you are and what you're about at a high level. Each new piece of content—be it a web page, marketing email, social media post, etc.—should refer back to your brand messaging guidelines.

WHAT KIND OF MUSIC SHOULD REPRESENT YOUR BRAND?

With the exploding popularity of smart speakers, podcasts, and live audio streams, a new form of brand building has emerged: *sonic branding.*

While most companies' brand identities remain overwhelmingly visual, more marketers are coming around to the idea that their brand should have a specific sonic signature—a kind of aural tagline.

Some brands have taken things a step further. In June of this year, Mastercard released its first album of original music, featuring songs incorporating "the recognizable melody of Mastercard's brand sound."

What kind of music should your brand choose to incorporate in the user experience? The answer depends on your audience.

How Music Inspires Trust

We all know that music inspires feelings in its listeners; it also increases our oxytocin levels. While this hormone is most closely associated with love, it also makes it easier for us to trust.

That means if you are a company looking for new ways to build trust in your brand, your choice of music is important.

Here's how to select the best music to instill trust in your buyers:

#1: Start with Your Brand Identity

Your brand's essence is the emotional benefit your company or product delivers. For ADT, it is peace of mind, for example, while for Red Bull, it is energy. The music you use should reflect your brand's essence.

Multiple studies confirm that consumers' musical genre preferences can be sorted into four qualitative categories:

- Reflective and complex (classical, jazz, folk, blues)
- Intense and rebellious (rock, alternative, heavy metal)
- Upbeat and conventional (country, pop, soundtracks, religious)

- Energetic and rhythmic (rap, soul, electronica)

One of those four can be a starting point for mapping music to your brand identity.

#2: Align Your Genre Choice with Buyer Demographics

Let's say your brand is an upstart innovator that is disrupting its industry. You might want to choose music that is "rebellious" to highlight this trait.

But how do you choose between rock, alternative, and heavy metal? That's where demographic information can be helpful.

Are your brand's buyers typically aged forty-five to fifty-four? In that case, you might wish to go with classic rock, which is more popular than alternative or metal with that age group.

#3: Take into Account Buyer Interests and Values

Just as you should take your target customers' demographics into account, you should also consider their values and interests. If you're marketing alternative-lifestyle products, for example, the Billboard Hot 100 is not likely to be the best soundtrack for your message.

Let's take the alignment with buyer values a step further. Say your business sells sustainable or locally sourced products. Many indie artists are committed to the cause of sustainability and attract audiences who are as well. You might consider teaming with one of these artists to promote your product through a music-driven campaign.

#4: Pick a Genre and Stick with It

Audiences tend to identify strongly with their favorite musical genres, so when you change your brand's music, your buyers might think of you differently.

A fascinating Australian study, published in the journal *PLOS ONE*, gave participants a set of song lyrics and asked them what emotions the lyrics elicited. The twist was that the song's genre was described differently to different participants. Some were told the lyrics were from an opera, while others were told they were from a hip-hop song, heavy metal song, or samba.

The researchers found that participants had varying emotional reactions to the lyrics simply based on this information. When participants thought the lyrics were part of a samba, they evoked happiness. When they thought they were from a hip-hop or metal song, they elicited anger (Susino 2020).

The lesson for marketers is that even a consistent message can be perceived as *in*consistent if the musical accompaniment changes.

#5: Choose Music That Inspires Positive Emotions

Once you've landed on a musical style that aligns with your brand's essence and your customers' preferences, you can focus on the individual song, soundtrack, or arrangement.

While the specific emotions you wish to inspire may vary from project to project, your best bet for instilling trust is to choose music that evokes positive emotions, because music that creates joy also builds trust.

#6: Match Tempo to Desired Actions

To gain buyer trust, you must align music not only with your brand, but also with your desired customer experience.

If you have a fast-casual restaurant, for example, music with a fast tempo is the best match for the experience because it leads to faster table turnover, so patrons don't have to wait as long to be seated. Chill music, by contrast, works better for supermarkets, because it encourages visitors to relax and explore the entire store.

#7: Let Music Drive the Action

Marketing works best when all the elements of your branding are tightly coordinated. While music is a valuable tool on its own, it is even more impactful when it helps tell your company or product's story.

Research has shown that music in television commercials, for example, becomes more memorable when it drives the ad's narrative—through tempo, lyrics, or other means.

#8: Choose a Recognizable Song to Increase Authority

Using a hit song in your marketing can carry a hefty price tag, but it can be worth it because of the value it delivers.

One of the key benefits of choosing recognizable music is authority; your buyers will trust you more simply by virtue of your association with a popular song by a famous artist. It is comparable to an influencer endorsement in the goodwill it generates.

#9: Evoke and Inspire Memories

Studies have consistently shown that music has a powerful link with our memory; it's why singing helps us learn a foreign language faster, for example.

One reason why choosing a recognizable song has real value in marketing is that it can take us back in time. It's why you crank up the volume when you come across a hit song from when you were a teenager; for a moment, you feel like that teen again. Brands can capture and associate themselves with these feelings, building a bond of affection and trust with buyers.

The moment you add music to your organization's marketing mix, it becomes part of your brand. Make sure your musical choices inspire customer trust.

Strategy #3: Full-Funnel Content

So far, we've discussed two important user-experience strategies, trust-centered website design and owned media. Now let's take a look at the third: full-funnel content strategy.

While an owned-media strategy assesses, prioritizes, and executes the best company-managed vehicles to promote trust, a full-funnel content strategy zeroes in on a single key aspect of owned media: *your content as it relates to the buyer's journey through the marketing funnel.*

Many books and articles on inbound marketing focus almost exclusively on the content that brands create themselves—as if this content lived in a vacuum. The marketing funnel, as imagined in this scenario, might work like this:

1. The buyer conducts a Google search and finds an article on your blog that addresses a problem they are seeking a solution for.
2. The buyer likes the blog article, so they subscribe to your email list.
3. The buyer receives an email featuring a video demo of your product or service and watches it.
4. The buyer is retargeted with an ad offering a 20-percent discount code for purchases made that day.
5. The buyer clicks through the ad to a landing page where they sign up and pay for your product or service.

I'm sure you've seen stages in the purchase funnel presented this way before. But had you ever noticed before that these were *all examples of owned media*?

That's not how buying really works. We've learned in this book that consumers trust what other people say about you more than what you say about yourself.

A more common funnel experience in 2022 would be this:

1. The buyer conducts a Google search and finds a helpful article by you, but it's in an industry trade publication, not your own blog.
2. When the buyer has an interest in the product or service you offer, they go to an industry review site and begin comparing their options. The buyer sees your brand name and recognizes it from the article you wrote, so they include you in their consideration set.

3. Because you have the best reviews among your competitors, the buyer looks for other information about you. They find media coverage highlighting your company's growth and successes.

4. The buyer finally decides to go to your website and purchase your product or service—*visiting your owned media for the first time in the buying process.*

Some inbound marketing firms only offer full-funnel content marketing, combined with a heavy dose of advertising, in their campaigns. It's important to understand that without integrating third-party validation from trusted sources, this insular approach is doomed to failure.

Specific Messages for Each Stage of the Buyer's Journey

That doesn't mean that a full-funnel content strategy isn't important. To borrow a supply-chain term, it supports the "last mile" to the sale—the last leg of the journey from awareness to trust to purchase.

While 95 percent of your buyers are *future* buyers—those not looking for your product or service at the moment—the other 5 percent are *now* buyers. Full-funnel content marketing is directed at now buyers, arguably your most important single audience.

As now buyers are drawn into your funnel, your owned media can finally begin to focus on selling your product.

The success of a full-funnel strategy hinges on *relevance*. Customers require unique messaging and creative forms of content at every stage of the funnel, so it's important for you to fine-tune your communications based on your knowledge of your buyer. This is where buyer persona research can prove invaluable.

Worry Less about Frequency, More about Relevance

Many marketers tend to obsess over tactics rather than strategies when developing and implementing their inbound marketing programs. That's often because they don't have a strategy that has been substantiated by buyer research.

Take the issue of communications frequency, for example. Too many marketers worry endlessly about questions like these:

- How often should I send out the newsletter?
- How far apart should my campaign emails be?
- When should I post on social media?
- How aggressively should I retarget my website visitors with ads?

But frequency isn't what matters to buyers; relevance is.

If you deliver relevant messages to your audience—messages that show you know what they're interested in, as well as where they are in the buying process—your buyers will tolerate a high frequency of communication.

If you don't, even one message may be one too many.

Today, we live in a world where consumers have grown to expect personalized offers, recommendations, and experiences when they interact with your brand. They expect you to *get* them.

If you can't provide your buyers with that feeling, they ultimately will lose trust in you—and you will lose the sale in the process.

As we discussed in Chapter 8 in examining the causes of ecommerce cart abandonment, a customer can drop out of the sales process at any time—even the last minute. The key is to continue to build trust with the buyer at every stage of the journey.

The Power of Personalization

One of the best ways to show relevance is *personalization.*

Personalization, at its essence, is simply taking what you already have learned about your buyer to create a better experience for them. Done well, that builds trust.

Personalization is a trust signal not only because it makes your buyer's shopping experience easier; it creates an emotional connection as well. Being treated as an individual, and not just a potential purchase, resonates with buyers.

According to a 2020 Deloitte study, 80 percent of buyers prefer brands that offer a personalized experience ("Connecting with Meaning"). And a majority of marketers report that personalization increases open rates and click-through rates for emails, as well as time on site and conversions for website visitors.

Simple strategies that go a long way include the following:

- Adding a welcome message for return website visitors
- Changing your website calls to action based on where your visitors are in the buying cycle
- Collecting information from email or website surveys that are then used to tailor communications
- Personalizing your emails and having them come from a real person rather than *noreply@companyname.com*
- Changing your website and email content dynamically based on the buyer's demonstrated interests
- Sending birthday or anniversary emails, along with a special offer, to spur additional purchases by existing customers

If you can create a full-funnel strategy that communicates a real understanding of your audience, you will satisfy a deep craving for your buyers—and they will reward you for it.

When Does Personal Become Too Personal?

Of course, we've all heard stories of personalized experiences that go too far or are otherwise cringe-worthy:

- A man chatting online about a family member with a serious illness, who starts seeing ads for funeral homes
- A teenage girl who is served ads for baby clothes before she's even told her parents she's pregnant
- A website suggesting that a food order doesn't fit a visitor's diet or that a purchase is not within their budget

When you collect visitor information, it's critical that you handle it with care. If you use it in a tone-deaf or invasive way, you will scare off customers. While consumers tend to push privacy questions to the backs of their minds, when confronted with them directly, 86 percent say they worry about how brands collect and use their data, according to a 2021 KPMG survey (Whitney 2021).

One of the best ways for marketers to make personalization less unsettling for consumers is to be transparent about it. Explain why you are collecting their information and why they are seeing a specific ad or having a specific experience with your content.

Ultimately, the advice here is simple, if easier said than done:

Provide the most relevant, personalized buyer experience possible. *But don't be creepy about it.*

It's a brand lesson even titans of business like Jeff Bezos are struggling with today.

CHAPTER 14

Getting Found— Search Presence

→ Earning media coverage is the single best way to tell Google your site is important; that's the job of Digital PR.

→ Technical and on-page SEO ensure your site gets credit for the content, coverage, and relationships you establish online.

→ Google is not just a search engine but the destination for most queries. That makes on-SERP optimization a must.

In 2015, as Google's algorithms slowly compelled the fields of PR and SEO to join forces, I gave the same talk at two events: the popular SEO conference State of Search and the Public Relations Society of America's Counselors Academy.

My presentation was titled, "The Shotgun Wedding of PR and SEO: Can This Marriage Be Saved?"

For practitioners in both industries, it *was* a shotgun wedding —the bride and groom lurching reluctantly toward each other with the blunderbuss of Google's algorithmic imperatives pointed squarely at them.

It used to be that PR practitioners could deliver SEO value simply by including links in press releases. Most didn't know—or didn't *want* to know—much about search marketing beyond that.

SEO practitioners, meanwhile, had little interest in brand building or PR. They were technical specialists focused on cracking Google's code to increase web traffic and sales for their clients. Landing the top ranking for high-volume keywords was all that mattered; the quality of the content—i.e., whether their client actually *deserved* that ranking—was a secondary consideration at best.

Google's releases of the Panda, Penguin, and Hummingbird algorithm updates in 2011, 2012, and 2013, respectively, changed all that. The updates killed the SEO value of press-release links, sending PR firms scrambling for other ways to show their digital worth. And it put SEO practitioners on notice that the search giant's number-one priority was to rank the highest-quality content with the highest-quality links as the top results. Game playing would no longer be tolerated.

Google added the icing to the cake the following year, with the introduction of the E-A-T formula in its Search Quality Rater

Guidelines. E-A-T is an acronym defining what Google values most in web content:

- Expertise
- Authoritativeness
- Trustworthiness

Google has been working relentlessly to align what ranks highest with what website visitors trust most ever since. Which is why integrating your PR and SEO strategies is one of the best ways to build, grow, and protect your brand today.

SEARCH-PRESENCE STRATEGIES TO BUILD AND GROW TRUST

SEO is about more than increasing traffic. A poor search presence tells your customers that your website is unimportant and that your brand lacks credibility with Google. It's like having your fancy office in a run-down neighborhood; it's not a good way to establish trust.

To *gain* Google's trust, your search presence strategy should include the following components:

1. **Digital PR strategy.** Google has confirmed that Digital PR is the best way to build links and authority for your website.
2. **Technical and on-page SEO strategy.** Digital PR only works, however, if your website is optimized to take advantage of it.
3. **Zero-click SEO strategy.** More than half of all Google searches never result in a click. That's why it is important

to make sure your brand stands out on Google's results pages, so your details are displayed and visible for users who don't click.

Let's explore each of these elements in more detail.

Strategy #1: Digital PR

John Mueller, Google's chief search advocate, said last year that when ranking websites, a single, high-value link from a major news website like *USA Today* or *The Wall Street Journal* carries more weight than "millions" of low-quality links (Southern 2021).

Think about that. It means that a single high-profile PR placement could have a greater impact on your search presence than all the efforts of your SEO firm over the past five years.

Google has made clear that combining PR and SEO is the most effective—and least spammy—search strategy of all.

This discipline has become known as *Digital PR*.

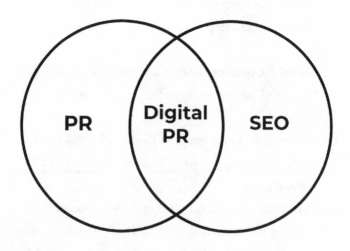

Traditional PR focuses on promoting brand awareness through media coverage. Digital PR, by contrast, focuses on promoting *linkable assets*—website content that is purposely crafted to attract links, usually from other sites in your niche. The site might be an industry trade, or it might be a blog by a company that is not a direct competitor but is also in your space.

A successful *traditional PR* campaign for a company announcement might earn twenty mentions in different media outlets over a period of days or weeks.

A successful *Digital PR* campaign promoting a linkable asset, by contrast, might earn *two hundred* links from a wide range of relevant websites—from high-profile media sites to small blogs— over a period of weeks, months, or years.

How to Create and Promote Linkable Assets

Linkable assets are the cornerstone of any Digital PR campaign. For a year-round Digital PR program, you should plan to produce at least one of these every quarter. Expect to spend six to eight weeks to research and develop the asset, then four to six weeks to promote it.

The type of linkable asset that tends to work best is a business or industry report that contains original research. You can collect this research from your own data (the B2B review site TrustRadius, for example, reports on the technology services and sectors that are most in demand based on its website traffic), or you can conduct surveys, either of your own customer base or working with third-party research companies.

Additional types of linkable assets include calculators, quizzes, and other interactive tools and assessments.

The process for creating and promoting a linkable asset generally goes like this:

#1: Research Your Topic

Use Google News, SEO keyword tools, and social media hashtags to surface the topics that are hot. Then, find an angle that fills a gap in coverage.

#2: Create and Optimize Your Asset

Develop a substantive piece of content that lives on your website and has been optimized to rank for a specific set of keywords for your chosen topic.

#3: Pitch the Story to High-Value Publications

Start several weeks before you publish your content to gain advance interest from key journalists. Give them materials under embargo, so they can prepare a story to run on the publication date.

#4: Begin to Rank for High-Volume Search Terms

If you've planned well, your initial coverage should help you rank for your target keywords. This will attract more eyeballs to your work, including some from other bloggers and journalists researching the topic.

#5: Earn Relevant Backlinks over Time

Ranking high in search results will lead to more backlinks for your content weeks, months, and even years into the future. It's the gift that keeps on giving.

Traditional PR measures the success of a campaign by the number of brand mentions in the media. Digital PR, by contrast, may generate links that do not reference your brand's name; a blog might direct its visitors to your asset with anchor text like "study" or "calculator," for example.

But these links can have an enormous impact on your brand's search presence—which is just as important to earning trust as even the highest-profile media mention.

Strategy #2: Technical and On-Page SEO

Imagine you are running a relay race. Going fast is important—but no matter how fast you run, if you botch the handoff of the baton, it's over. You'll never win the race.

That's how it is with Digital PR and your website. No matter how much work you put into link outreach, you won't be successful if you don't align it closely with technical and on-page optimization. The handoff from off-site SEO to on-site SEO is critical.

Technical SEO refers to improving the technical aspects of a website, encompassing trust signals such as site security, page speed, navigability, and clean coding. It also includes adding structured data to your site, which makes it easier for Google to highlight your content in search results.

In 2021, Google introduced *Core Web Vitals*, which measure your site's load times, interactivity, and visual stability. Google describes Core Web Vitals as "signals that are essential to delivering a great user experience on the web." Google provides guidance to developers in helping websites achieve these standards.

Matching the Keyword with the Experience

On-page SEO focuses on improving the content, organization, and internal linking strategy of your site to enhance search presence.

Deploying a keyword strategy is a starting point for on-page SEO—but it's only a starting point. As Google puts it in its "How Search Works" report:

> The most basic signal that information is relevant is when a webpage contains the same keywords as your search query. If those keywords appear on the same page, or if they appear in the headings or body of the text, the information is more likely to be relevant.
>
> Beyond simple keyword matching, we use aggregated and anonymized interaction data to assess whether search results are relevant to queries. We transform that data into signals that help our machine-learned systems better estimate relevance. ("How Search Works: Ranking Results")

So Google looks to your use of keywords in your content, page URL, page title, headers, and meta description to determine what your page is about. Then, it looks at user experience data to determine whether visitors are satisfied with your page when they land on it—or if they go somewhere else instead.

Expect Google's ability to evaluate—and rank—your site based on user experience to only increase in the years ahead.

Strategy #3: Zero-Click SEO

If you think Google's primary purpose is to serve as a search engine that directs visitors to other websites, it might surprise you to learn that as many as 65 percent of searches do not result in a click at all, according to a 2021 study by Similarweb (Nguyen 2021). These users never leave Google's *search engine results pages*, or SERPs.

And that's exactly the way Google wants it.

Over the past several years, the number of so-called "zero-click" searches has increased sharply as Google has introduced more and more features to its SERPs that keep people in the Googleverse. This trend is even more pronounced on mobile devices, where as many as three-quarters of all searches are zero-click, according to the Similarweb study.

This study confirms what we should all know by now: Google is not just a way station but a *destination* for web visitors. That means brands would be wise to treat it like a media platform in their PR and SEO efforts—one that is hungry for your content.

With a few exceptions, Google does not produce its own content. It repurposes content created by others, which it displays on its SERPs. Its sources range from global news organizations to the smallest business and personal websites. This is how it generates more than $150 billion per year in advertising revenues.

Google SERP Features

So, how do you get your brand more exposure on Google results pages? Beyond overall search optimization, it's critical to understand and maximize your opportunity to appear on Google SERP features—widgets that appear above or alongside organic results.

These include:

- **Featured snippets.** Answers to questions that appear in the coveted "position zero" on a search page. They can be paragraphs, lists, tables, or videos. (e.g., "What are the benefits of PR?")
- **Instant answers.** Quick answers to simple questions, typically verified by search results (e.g., "How many inches are in a yard?")

- **Definitions.** For queries involving words—their definition, meaning, and usage (e.g., "What is a paradox?")
- **Map results.** For queries involving directions or distance. (e.g., "How long will it take to drive from Dallas to Chicago?")
- **Calculator.** For queries involving math (e.g., "What is 75 percent of 1,564?")
- **Knowledge panels.** These typically appear in the top right corner of search results and include information about the topic or brand. For brands with physical locations, a Google Business Profile is a feature that companies can claim and largely control.

Now that you know all this, what can *you* do to master the zero-click search?

WHY A GOOGLE BUSINESS PROFILE IS A MUST
FOR YOUR SEARCH PRESENCE

When people search for your company by name, think of that first page of results as your "second home page." What do your buyers and other audiences see? One of the best ways to greet them is with a Google Business Profile.

A Google Business Profile (formerly Google My Business) is a must for any business with physical locations customers can visit.

To create a profile, start by submitting your business name, location, and category to Google. Once your identity is verified, your profile will be created. You can create a profile wherever you have a physical business location.

After your profile is up and running, add photos, events, and other updates to make it stand out. As part of your listing, Google also lets consumers add feedback, reviews, and photos; ask questions; and even provide answers to certain questions about your business.

Google Maps and Reviews

When you create a Google Business Profile listing, your business will begin appearing in Google Maps. This is helpful when people search for you by name and want to visit you—but it's even more valuable when users are seeking the products and services you offer.

According to Google, nearly half of all searches have local intent. That's why when someone seeks out "accounting firms" or "plumbers," Google Maps displays the closest providers near the user's location, with the top three results highlighted. Being part of the so-called "Google 3-Pack" is great for trust and even better for traffic.

Google reviews and star ratings also appear in your Google Business Profile and Google Maps results, making them the most prominent customer reviews of local businesses by far. So be sure to ask for and respond to these reviews regularly.

Rich Results and Structured Data

Google classifies much of the content that appears in snippets and other SERP features as *rich results*, or enhanced organic search results. It provides guidance on how brands can best position their website content to be highlighted in these results.

Specifically, Google instructs marketers to implement structured data markup on their sites. Structured data is a standardized format for providing information about a page and classifying its content. Google advises developers on the proper markup for different rich result types, such as datasets, event information, recipes, and so forth.

The majority of websites today use at least some structured data, but few are as well-optimized as they could be, because most marketers leave this task to developers or content-management-system plug-ins rather than rolling up their sleeves and getting involved themselves.

That's a missed opportunity. Putting this in traditional PR terms, appearing in Google's SERP features can be thought of as a media placement. Adding the right structured data markup to your most important content is your way of "pitching" the search engine. It's worth the effort.

PR and SEO came together several years ago in a marriage that could only be described as awkward. But today, it is a productive partnership—and one that should grow even more lucrative for brands and practitioners over time. The Grow With TRUST system offers a straightforward way to leverage these synergies, with a focus on Digital PR. As Google itself has confirmed, it's the best way to improve your search presence.

CHAPTER 15

Sharing Knowledge— Thought Leadership

→ B2B buyers consume a lot of thought leadership content, but judge only 15 percent to be of high quality.

→ Stand out by finding a niche, voice, and purpose. Don't create content about your product—but do create it for your buyers.

→ Publish content where it will be seen by your audience— on social media, on your website, and in trusted publications and blogs.

According to the Oxford English Dictionary, the term "thought leader" dates back to an 1887 biography of the abolitionist Henry Ward Beecher, who the authors called "one of the great thought-leaders in America" (Pratt 2018).

The concept of thought leadership was popularized in the 1990s by economist Joel Kurtzman, co-founder of the magazine *Strategy+Business*.

Kurtzman defined the term this way:

> A thought leader is recognized by peers, customers and industry experts as someone who deeply understands the business they are in, the needs of their customers and the broader marketplace in which they operate. They have distinctively original ideas, unique points of view and new insights. (Hall 2019)

This description has held up pretty well for nearly three decades. Unfortunately, the mantle of thought leadership has become so sought-after that it has led to a content glut.

Most B2B marketing executives today list positioning their company as a thought leader as one of their top objectives. The web now claims 600 million blogs, with 32 million active bloggers in the United States alone, according to Statista. And marketers that publish more frequently are rewarded; blogs that post four times a week get 3.5 times the traffic of those that publish only once per week (Connell 2022).

That doesn't mean you should get caught up on the content hamster wheel, however. And you shouldn't get discouraged, either.

Because the worst-kept secret in marketing is that most thought leadership content is *crap*.

WHY BAD THOUGHT LEADERSHIP IS WORSE
THAN NONE AT ALL

Done well, thought-leadership marketing can be highly effective in building your brand and growing your business. Here are some numbers from a 2020 Edelman survey to prove the point ("2020 B2B Thought Leadership Impact Study"):

- Nearly 50 percent of B2B decision-makers spend an hour or more each week consuming thought leadership content. They are looking for insights.
- Eighty-nine percent say that thought leadership affects their perception of an organization.
- Nearly 50 percent say that thought leadership impacts their buying decisions.

However, there is another number from that survey that should give every marketer pause:

- Only 15 percent consider the thought leadership they are consuming to be of high quality.

Content has always been about a transaction. The person consuming the content agrees to give you their time, and, in exchange, you agree to give them something worthy of that time. Too many marketers have forgotten the second half of that equation.

THOUGHT LEADERSHIP STRATEGIES TO EARN TRUST

In this chapter we'll be covering thought leadership in the Grow With TRUST model, focusing on the following elements:

1. **Thought leadership platform.** Thought leadership starts with having valuable ideas, knowledge, and advice to share that tie back to your brand and set you apart from competitors.
2. **Contributed content strategy.** Bylined articles and other forms of contributed content are a chance to share your expertise in the publications your audiences read and respect.
3. **Executive visibility strategy.** There are no shortcuts to establishing yourself on social media—but if you've targeted your channels well, the rewards are worth the effort.

Let's get started.

Strategy #1: Thought Leadership Platform

I can't tell you how many clients I've counseled about thought leadership platforms who've responded, *"But I don't have anything to say."*

I've found they almost always do—if they give themselves the time to think about it. Finding a niche, purpose, and point of view is within almost every brand's grasp.

That's where your thought leadership strategy should start.

You may have heard that every snowflake is different, and it's true—no matter how many billions of them fall from the sky, no two are ever the same. No one has the same work and life experiences as your brand's executives. Once they get the hang of it, they'll realize they have a lot more to say than they thought.

What's Your Second Sentence?

There's a question that newspaper editorial writers often ask each other during the ideation process: *"What's your second sentence?"*

This typically is asked when a writer is tasked with opining about something where the takeaway is rather obvious.

Something horrible or tragic happened? We are sad.

Something wonderful happened? We are happy!

Well, of course you are. But what's the second sentence? People expect more than the obvious from those editorial writers. They expect a personal, unique perspective.

The same question needs to be asked before your brand establishes a thought leadership platform.

Your brand's audience expects more than the obvious, too. They expect more than a sales piece. They expect a point of view.

And this point of view—while non-branded—should align strategically with your brand story. Unfortunately, many branding firms don't include thought leadership messaging in their engagements. That leads to brand guidelines that don't extend to thought leadership marketing.

A thought leadership platform identifies narratives and themes that fit neatly within a set of three considerations:

1. The brand's overall messaging and identity
2. Business or industry trends and themes that align with the brand's differentiation and vision
3. Executive or subject-matter expert (SME) spokesperson(s) with expertise and passion for these topics

Remember, there are two types of buyers: now buyers and future buyers—and the latter group is much larger than the former. A thought leadership marketing strategy builds trust with future buyers, so when they are ready to buy, they'll think of you first.

Beyond connecting with buyers, thought leadership also shows you have ideas to share and value to provide freely to others, which helps to establish a positive reputation online.

Invest Your Brain and Your Time—or Don't Bother

While most companies like the *idea* of thought leadership marketing, many simply aren't willing to follow through with the time and effort necessary to be successful. Company thought leaders are typically company leaders—CEOs, CMOs, CIOs. Their time is valuable and usually already accounted for.

For this reason, in-house marketers often try to find ways to produce thought leadership content without taking up their executives' time. This is almost always a mistake. Yes, a brand's PR firm or marketing team can *ghostwrite* the article. But the executive's unique insights are what make it authentic thought leadership.

Unfortunately, I've had the following conversation (or variations of it) too many times:

Client: "Our CEO doesn't have time to talk with you right now for the thought leadership piece."

Me: "Oh, really? Because we can't write it without interviewing her."

Client: "Well...uh...can't you just take these pieces of collateral, those blog posts, and this internal document and create something—and then put her name on it?"

Me: "Can we? Yes. But should we? No."

Client: "Why not?"

Me: "Because that's aggregation and regurgitation—not thought leadership."

In other words, we may be able to come up with a very compelling *first* sentence—but we still won't have a second.

Creating a thought leadership platform begins at the second sentence. It begins when you break away from the chorus of voices in your industry all saying the same things. It begins when you move past the obvious and start offering value and perspective that align with your brand's story and purpose.

The design-software company Autodesk, for example, started out as the company behind AutoCAD, the popular computer-aided design software. Over time, it has steadily expanded its vision and product offerings—and now proclaims that its bold mission is to "change how the world is designed and made."

Autodesk's thought leadership platform aligns neatly with this brand narrative. Its online magazine, *Redshift*, states that its charter is "to explore the future of how products, buildings, and cities will be built tomorrow—and even 100 years from now." *Redshift* is packed with helpful resources for B2B buyers of all sizes and skill levels.

That's how to provide value, instill a brand message—and build trust with both your now and future buyers.

THE TAO OF THOUGHT LEADERSHIP

Two decades ago, sisters Jenniphr and Greer Goodman created a wonderful indie film called *The Tao of Steve* about a slovenly, under-achieving kindergarten teacher named Dex (played by Donal Logue), who, despite his imperfections, had developed a surefire strategy for wooing women who most assumed were out of his league.

As he explained to one of his astonished friends, the strategy —inspired by Dex's idol, '70s movie star Steve McQueen—was simple. It included three steps:

1. *Be desireless*—focus on getting to know the person; don't make it about romance right away.
2. *Be excellent*—prove your worthiness by showing off something you're really good at—juggling, card tricks, art history, whatever.
3. *Be gone*—because, as Dex puts it, "We pursue that which retreats from us."

When I watched the movie again recently, it occurred to me that Dex's Tao (or method) applies not only to dating, but also to businesses seeking to woo customers with thought leadership. Here's how:

- **Be desireless.** Thought leadership is not about selling; it's about helping. If you can't separate the two in your mind when creating your content, you shouldn't bother creating it. Sharing interesting and useful information with those who come across your brand online is one of the best ways to establish rapport and build trust. It shows that you have more to offer the world than a product to sell. For top-of-the-funnel audiences, talking about your ideas more and your products less (or not at all) is the way to impress.

- **Be excellent.** How do you stand out with thought leadership? Not by posting more content than everyone else, but by seeming *smarter* than everyone else. Your content will be deemed excellent only when it is highly attuned to the needs, desires, interests, and predispositions of your target audience. The more you've researched your audience, the better you will know them and the smarter your content will seem to them.

- **Be gone.** Because thought leadership marketing is mostly a top-of-the-funnel activity, your buyers usually aren't ready to buy when they come across your content. It may be a year or more before they are ready to replace that enterprise software or can get out of their current service contract. So you will likely turn them off if you are too aggressive in your follow-up. Sign them up for your blog, retarget them with advertising, as long as you're not too annoying about it, and then count on them to remember your desirelessness and excellence when the time comes.

In the battle for attention amid a growing glut of mediocre content, it might be tempting to be more salesy and aggressive to stand out from your competitors. But as Dex can tell you, the better path is to be desireless, be excellent, and be gone.

Strategy #2: Contributed Content

Once you have your thought leadership platform in place, the next step is to figure out how to find an audience for your content.

A natural place to start is with your owned media, such as your blog, podcast, or social media channels. But it's also important to extend your thought leadership to outside audiences—those who have not yet discovered your brand or website. One of the best ways to do this is by earning *bylined article* placements in the publications your buyers respect and consume.

The journalism term "byline" first appeared in print with the publication of Ernest Hemingway's *The Sun Also Rises* in 1926. Hemingway spelled it "by-line," which makes sense; it denotes the line atop a newspaper or magazine article stating who the piece is "by"—the author. Originally used to ensure accountability for mistakes in reporting, the byline, over time, has become one of the most sought-after status symbols among journalists—turning columnists into celebrities and investigative reporters into trusted community watchdogs.

Bylined articles, in other words, have a storied history. That's why when brands treat contributed content as just another PR or SEO tactic, they are doing themselves a disservice.

Done well, bylined articles can be your single most effective inbound marketing strategy. In fact, they can achieve a Grow With TRUST trifecta, not only advancing your thought leadership efforts, but also contributing to your third-party validation and search presence.

Here's how:

- Bylines bring visibility to your company's thought leadership, and thought leadership builds trust.
- Placing a byline in a well-known publication delivers the benefit of third-party validation, because that outlet confers trust on your brand by choosing to publish your content.
- Bylined articles—especially those with links to your brand's website—yield important benefits for search presence; and high visibility in Google also builds trust.

Maximizing and balancing each of these benefits is the three-legged stool of a contributed-content strategy.

The Guest-Post Trap

In the SEO world, bylined articles are more popularly known by another name: *guest posts.*

Unfortunately, guest posting has taken a reputation hit in recent years—mostly because of marketers publishing poor-quality content, often in paid linking schemes, in order to accumulate backlinks. In 2014, Google raised a red flag about guest posting, when its search-quality spokesman, Matt Cutts (2014), wrote a post titled, "The decay and fall of guest blogging for SEO."

Cutts stated at the time:

Back in the day, guest blogging used to be a respectable thing, much like getting a coveted, respected author to write the introduction of your book...(but) if you're using guest blogging as a way to gain links in 2014, you should probably stop. Why? Because over time it's become a more and more spammy practice...

Google later clarified that not all guest posting is bad—but to this day, the search giant says it frowns on it as a link-building strategy and devalues guest-post links it considers "unnatural."

This means that you should focus on creating great thought leadership content first—and then securing publication of that content in high-authority media outlets that Google trusts.

If you do, the SEO benefits will come...*naturally*.

BYLINED ARTICLE PROGRAM CHECKLIST

Contributed content can require a significant amount of time to plan, write, and pitch to the media. Below is a ten-point checklist to follow when creating a bylined article for a brand executive or SME:

1. Start by referencing the brand's thought leadership platform to guide the content development process.
2. Brainstorm on topics, trends, and story ideas to share with the exec or SME to whom the article will be attributed.
3. Interview the exec or SME to learn their perspective on the topic; then, transcribe the interview to be able to include their insights directly in the piece.
4. Identify publications and blogs your audience trusts that accept contributed articles.
5. Use editorial calendars to determine when publications will be most receptive to specific story ideas.
6. Consider timing to align publication dates with company initiatives or announcements.

7. Explore sponsored content opportunities offered by *Forbes, Fast Company, Entrepreneur,* and others.

8. Create a brief article abstract and pitch to the media before writing the full piece.

9. Once the abstract is accepted, draft the full article and get approval from the exec or SME to submit.

10. Promote your article on social media, on your website, and through paid advertising once it has been published.

Establishing your brand and its executives as thought leaders through a bylined article program takes brainpower, patience, and commitment—but it's an effective strategy for earning brand trust.

Strategy #3: Executive Visibility

Thought leadership marketing is a partnership between a brand and its executives. Raising the profile of your CEO and other company leaders—the spokespeople for your thought leadership platform—increases the authority and authenticity of your brand for audiences.

A January 2020 study in *Qualitative Market Research* used focus groups to assess the perception of CEOs as company spokespeople. The study concluded that putting a CEO in front of consumers "sends a positive signal and creates a human-to-human connection."

As one participant told the researchers:

It's a human speaking to another human. The presence of the CEO brings life, you can see a face, a style, a way of doing things...Putting a face on a brand name is somehow a way of saying "I want to connect with you." (Zeitoun, Michel, and Fleck-Dousteyssier 2020)

This conclusion is backed by the findings of Edelman's Trust Barometer surveys, which consistently show that corporate CEOs rank among the most trusted figures in American public life.

That's why an executive visibility strategy is an excellent investment for brands—and today, that starts with social media.

Unfortunately, many executive visibility programs never get off the ground because CEOs and other executives are so busy in their jobs that feeding the beast of social media seems like an impossible task.

That's where PR and marketing practitioners can help. These programs work best when they are a joint effort of the executive and the brand's marketing team or PR agency. With a clear thought leadership platform to work from, marketers can help their executives with setting up channels, posting content, building relationships, and more.

The Executive Thought Leader's Guide to Social Media

To get you started, here are seven steps to help your CEO build a thought leadership presence on social media:

#1: Choose the Right Channel

While it may sound appealing to spread your thought leadership all over the internet, from Reddit to TikTok, this can lead to a loss of focus and an inability to establish a foothold on any one site.

That's why a land-and-expand strategy is a better approach to your CEO's social media presence.

Experiment with three channels you'd like to build an audience on—LinkedIn, Twitter, and Quora are great options for B2B CEOs—and see where you begin to gain traction. Based on relationships, algorithms, and other factors, you may find the same content that falls flat on Twitter earns big engagement on LinkedIn. Lean into that strength and build on it to establish your CEO as a thought leader. Focus on that platform until you are successful and then expand your presence elsewhere.

#2: Share the Person Behind the Title

While your CEO may lead a well-known technology company that's always innovating, it's the person behind the brand who people typically connect with. This is where your CEO needs to open up and show how their interests, passions, and hobbies intersect with the brand. Your audience will see your CEO as more giving and authentic—and trustworthy.

#3: Don't Just Broadcast—Show Interest in Others

When someone in the social media world mentions your CEO or brand, share those mentions on your company's account and the CEO's personal account as well. To the extent the CEO makes time to answer questions, address concerns, acknowledge mentions, and share the content of others, it burnishes their reputation as an approachable executive. Social media is a "you scratch my back, I'll scratch yours" world, and if you want to attract consistent engagement, you have to consistently engage.

#4: Use Analytics to See What's Working

You shouldn't fly blind with your CEO's social media content—unless you want to leave success to chance. That's why it's important to invest in quality analytics tools, like Shield for LinkedIn or TrackMyHashtag for Twitter, to see what's working and what isn't. Study the subject matter of the executive's posts, the time of day they're sent, different hashtag strategies, and other variables to see what tends to increase visibility. Then, lean into that. Give the people what they want.

THOUGHT LEADERSHIP ON QUORA

It's not as sexy as TikTok or Twitter, but Quora is one of the top social networks—as well as one of the one hundred most-trafficked websites in the world. After LinkedIn, it is arguably the premier platform for thought leadership, with more than three hundred million monthly active users.

Quora is distinguished by its question-and-answer format, the basis for all engagement on the site. "Quorans," as members are known, have asked and answered millions of questions on topics ranging from personal to politics to business. An estimated three thousand to five thousand new questions are added to Quora daily. The most popular writers on Quora receive millions of views, upvotes, and shares of their content.

Interactions on Quora are demand-driven: people ask directly for your expertise and guidance. This includes many buyers—both B2C and B2B—who turn to the platform to self-educate.

Quora is a forum that can boost aspiring thought leaders in a number of ways:

1. Quora helps you gain authority and awareness in your industry when you answer questions, join groups, and participate in conversations. It's one of the best ways to get your ideas in front of a large audience quickly.

2. Answering Quora questions increases your visibility in Google searches, particularly for long-tail keywords that are specific to your business or industry. Your Quora answers can continue to draw interest over months or years.

3. Quora allows you to answer questions about your product, explain features, and overcome objections. This provides education for those who might be a little further down the marketing funnel.

After you set up your Quora profile, being personal and authentic is the key to gaining a following, emerging as a thought leader, and growing your business.

Some specific tips when getting started:

- Actively search for questions that you want to engage with and set them aside so you can work on them.

- Answer questions in an informative way that is not self-serving or salesy. Be helpful and contribute to conversations.

- Answer a mix of popular and niche questions to expand your audience while reinforcing your areas of specialization.

- Upvote, share, and comment on the answers of other Quorans to build a network of members with similar interests.
- Make your answers stand out by using images, videos, variations in font, and other techniques that Quorans use to make their answers visually appealing.

Quora prides itself on fostering a more civil form of discourse than other social media sites. You can delete comments on your answers if they are rude, irrelevant, or inappropriate.

Whatever your campaign's specific objectives, Quora offers helpful, intuitive analytics to track your progress.

Give it a try. It's a great way for executives to earn authority and trust with relevant audiences online.

#5: Only Post Content You Would Click on Yourself

The shelf life of a tweet today is about fifteen minutes. That's not much time to grab a user's attention, interest, or loyalty. Before posting on social media, your CEO and internal team should ask themselves, "Would I click on this content?" If the answer is "no" or "I'm not sure," it's unlikely the post will be appearing at the top of anyone's feed. You have to believe in your content first, before you can expect others to.

#6: Encourage Employee Ambassadors

Get your team involved in promoting your CEO's content, especially if your number-one platform is LinkedIn, where virtually all of your employees are likely to have a presence. Did you know LinkedIn claims to provide as many as 80 percent of social media leads for B2B companies? That's a number no brand can afford to ignore.

So, if you are beginning to find traction with a LinkedIn strategy, be sure to fully engage your team. Encourage them to share your CEO's posts on their personal LinkedIn pages—and to publish their own content, too. This will make your brand more visible and extend thought leadership to all levels of your organization.

#7: Amplify Your Content with Social Media Advertising

While growing your CEO's social media presence without advertising support is possible, it can be difficult and slow-going. Social media advertising accelerates the process of getting your content noticed. And it doesn't require breaking the bank; an effective thought leadership campaign can be run on a reasonable budget.

If you want your CEO or other top executives to stand out as thought leaders, an active social media presence is no longer optional. Give your audience what they want by choosing the right channel, sharing personal stories and interests, engaging followers with relevant content, and taking a genuine interest in others.

SAY SMART THINGS AND LEAVE THE
PRAISE TO OTHERS

Thought leadership is key to the Grow With TRUST system because it gives you something to talk about *besides* your product.

And nowhere is the benefit of that more obvious than on social media.

How often do you come across companies that program their Twitter or Facebook feeds like a TV show, complete with commercial breaks?

Here's how the formula might go for a B2B tech company on Twitter:

Tweet 1: Company summarizes and links to a trade media story sharing industry news

Tweet 2: Company summarizes and links to a channel partner's blog post offering perspective on an industry trend

Tweet 3: Company summarizes and links to an industry analyst's latest report

Tweet 4: Company highlights one of its product features and links to a demo or promotion

The brand publishes content to inform and entertain its audience —then, in the last tweet, makes the audience "pay the tax" of a product promotion.

That's the traditional advertising model.

And it runs directly counter to Grow With TRUST.

Because what the company in this example is actually doing is posting content from *other people* saying smart things about their industry—and from the brand *promoting itself*.

In the Grow With TRUST system, it's the opposite: you publish *your own leaders* saying smart things about the industry—and leave the promotion of your product to your *customers, influencers, and others*. Those are the two Ts in TRUST: third-party validation and thought leadership.

Thought leadership is the final part of the Grow With TRUST system. Now, let's turn to putting this system into practice.

CHAPTER 16

Getting Started with Grow With TRUST

→ Getting started with a Grow With TRUST program requires PR firms to look at their clients' goals in a new way.

→ Implementing the Grow With TRUST system requires cross-functional cooperation within brands and agencies.

→ The Grow With TRUST wish list is one way to prioritize competing initiatives within a cross-functional program.

"Everybody talks about the weather," Mark Twain is famously said to have remarked. "But no one does anything about it."

So it seems to be with trust these days. There is plenty of gnashing of teeth among marketers and communicators about how consumers are less trusting than they used to be. But where are the pragmatic solutions for improving trust between brands and their audiences? Mostly I see surveys and institutes and panel discussions —not practical guidance.

That's where trust signals come in. Trust signals are the tools that should fill every PR professional's toolkit. A modern public relations agency should be able to help its clients build a path of credibility—"breadcrumbs of trust"—to accelerate every aspect of the marketing funnel.

But having a list of trust signals to work from isn't enough; your business's trust-building efforts need to be part of a unified plan. That's where my Grow With TRUST system comes in. It brings together trust signals in an integrated set of solutions, all supported by strategies proven to help brands secure trust at scale.

While Grow With TRUST is designed to help any business, and can be deployed successfully by marketers, entrepreneurs, and others, I stated at the outset of *Trust Signals* that I created this framework with PR professionals in mind.

That's because Grow With TRUST can help PR agencies expand their services and grow their own businesses in a more organized way, with a more coherent rationale. The entire system is built around what PR firms do best: *helping brands secure trust at scale.*

SELLING GROW WITH TRUST
TO PR CLIENTS

When I share the Grow With TRUST system with my peers at other PR agencies, I am often told it won't be accepted by clients.

"When companies call us, they just want media coverage. They aren't open to other services," they say.

My team used to think that, too, until we began having different kinds of conversations with our clients and prospects—and began listening for clues that they wanted something more, too.

For example, when we ask prospects what they are hoping to achieve with media coverage, we often hear something like this:

"Buyers do their own research today, and we want them to see us in news coverage when they are doing this."

Now, when we get an answer like this, we could respond in one of two ways:

1. That's great, and we're happy to help you get that coverage; or
2. That's great, but what else do your buyers look for in their research, and how are you addressing that?

We used to settle for the first response. Give the people what they want, right?

Now we *always* ask the latter question. We'd rather show our clients what they *need*, and give them that, instead.

BUYERS AND DYOR

In the 1990s, conspiracy theorists on the web began using the phrase, "Do your own research," to encourage skepticism of the mainstream media and academic elites. With the emergence of QAnon and similar movements, the admonition to do your own research—or *DYOR*—has become more popular than ever.

But it's not DYOR about controversial topics like vaccines that has had the biggest impact on our society; it's DYOR about everything. A 2020 Pew Research Center survey showed that 81 percent of Americans rely "a lot" on doing their own research before making important decisions—with the internet being their number-one source of information. That's compared to 43 percent of Americans who rely on friends and family and only 31 percent who look to professional experts for advice (Turner and Rainie 2020).

As part of this shift to internet research, consumers have transitioned to a DYOR mentality when buying almost anything—from a pair of sneakers to multimillion-dollar enterprise software.

As we've learned throughout this book, the breadcrumb path to purchase is different for every individual and audience. That's why it's so important to invest in research to understand your buyers and the sources of influence they trust.

But based on what we know generally to be true, if a client is seeking to reach buyers who are doing their own research, will a couple of positive news stories be enough?

Would that article in *Parents* magazine have been enough to convince our account manager, Laurie Lane, to buy that crib mattress in Chapter 6?

No. For Laurie, the breadcrumb trail included, in addition to that *Parents* coverage:

- an Instagram creator, who introduced her to the brand;
- Google, which elevated the brand in search results;
- customers, who gave five-star reviews to the mattress online; and
- a celebrity athlete, who partnered with the brand.

This should come as no surprise to us. It's how internet research works.

So what are we actually doing for a prospect who comes to us in this environment and asks for media coverage—and we agree to do *only* that for them?

What we are *not* doing is helping them as we should—and in the way, with the right tools, organization, and mentality, that we *can*.

DEPLOYING A
CROSS-FUNCTIONAL SYSTEM

The Grow With TRUST framework sets forth a modern, integrated approach to the practice of PR. This can present implementation challenges for some agencies and brands—but it is worth the time and effort to overcome these.

In any cross-functional system, organizational silos can make working across disciplines—toward shared goals—difficult. The idea of PR, content, social media, design, and strategy working together seamlessly is a pipe dream in many organizations.

But it is a necessity for the Grow With TRUST system.

If you're a brand seeking an agency's help, make sure the firm is organized to make cross-functional cooperation as frictionless as possible. Every team member working for your brand—no matter their function—should speak with a single voice for you.

If you are a PR agency that would like to break down silos to offer the Grow With TRUST system to clients, the first step is to organize around solutions rather than capabilities. Grow With TRUST can't be implemented without a solution-centered approach.

For some agencies, that may require significant changes to your organizational chart—for others, simply a change of mindset.

SUPERMAN, FLASH, AND
THE INTEGRATED AGENCY ADVANTAGE

When I was a kid, I was a DC Comics guy. And that meant I loved Superman—the original superhero who had it all: super strength, X-ray and heat vision, invulnerability, super hearing, and "freeze" breath, just to name a few of his superpowers.

Superman was more powerful than a locomotive. He could leap tall buildings in a single bound. And he was faster than a speeding bullet.

That's pretty fast.

But after introducing Superman in 1938, DC later created the Flash, "the fastest man alive." And ever since then, comics aficionados of all ages have debated the eternal question, "Who's faster?"

This led to a series of races over the years—the first in 1967. Most of the races ended up in a tie; the others were narrow Flash victories.

Growing up, my perspective on those races was this: "Who cares if Flash is a little faster? Superman is the total package!"

And that's the rationale for choosing an integrated agency over a specialist firm. While the specialist firm might be better at certain things, an integrated firm is usually the better choice overall.

A Single, Strong Partner

Integrated agencies provide inherent advantages over going the specialist route. If I'm a CMO and I hire separate agencies for PR, social media, website design, brand strategy, SEO, and content marketing (to cite a rather extreme example), that's six different invoices to pay every month.

It's also six different times I have to repeat myself whenever the company's strategy changes or a big announcement is going out—or I just want to update everyone on *anything*.

I also have to deal with the fact that everything in digital marketing is inextricably linked today. Is it even possible to separate content from SEO, or social media from media relations? Not effectively.

And good luck having a consistent brand voice with so many mouthpieces. It just doesn't work.

Having a single, strong agency partner can also help a brand stay on track with its program.

Often, a client comes to Idea Grove with big goals. The CMO has been given a directive from above to do any number of things—improve awareness, increase site traffic, fill the sales funnel. We kick off a program for them, and for the first few months, that's what we work toward.

But then other things start to compete for the CMO's attention. Someone in sales asks for a new piece of collateral. Or the sales deck needs to be redesigned. Or they need a new page added to the website. And slowly, that singular focus on strategic goals gets blurred. The urgent overwhelms the important.

It's understandable. As a marketer, your table gets crowded. Your eye wanders. Or a directive from one leader starts to compete with a directive from another.

When that happens with my agency's clients, we consider it our job to direct focus back to those original strategic goals. That only works, though, when you have one strong agency partner who, like you, can see the big picture and step in to help.

All of this makes for a pretty good case for integration.

But what's the argument for hiring a PR firm, rather than a creative firm or performance-marketing firm or advertising agency, to lead the way?

My argument is the Grow With TRUST system—the PR-centric approach to brand building in a post-truth world.

DETERMINING PRIORITIES WITHIN GROW WITH TRUST

For brands implementing the Grow With TRUST system, all five solutions—third-party validation, reputation management, user experience, search presence, and thought leadership—are equally important to building, growing, and protecting a well-rounded brand.

But it can seem like a lot to take on all at once, particularly with a smaller marketing department or limited budget.

So what's the best place to get started?

It depends on the things you're already doing and the areas in which you're already strong, but in general you should prioritize the Grow With TRUST solutions as follows:

Priority #1: User Experience

All roads lead to your website, so if you aren't establishing trust here, your other efforts won't matter. When brands contact us about PR services, the first thing we do is analyze their website. If we don't believe the site is capable of building trust—for all the reasons discussed in Chapters 4, 5, and 13—we recommend the client update their site before considering a PR campaign.

Priority #2: Third-Party Validation

When your buyers do their research, the first thing they seek is validation from media, influencers, and customers. If they can't find that, they will question if you're legit. So ensuring that you have a steady cadence of positive reviews, influencer endorsements, and media coverage is critical to guiding consumers along the trust breadcrumb trail.

Priority #3: Search Presence

The best way to amplify your website and third-party endorsements is to enhance your search presence. That means developing social media profiles, review site profiles, and a Google Business Profile to appear high in search results when people look for you by name. It also means aligning your brand's content with the topics your buyers search for—and then attracting inbound links to that content so it will be more easily found.

Priority #4: Reputation Management

Protecting the trust you have built online requires an insurance policy for when things go sideways. Everything your brand has done up to this point—creating a great website, earning third-party validation, gaining traction in Google results—helps create a foundation that is easier to protect when criticism, complaints, and cancellations come for you. But you must also be ready to respond to bad press, negative reviews, and social media pile-ons at a moment's notice. If you're not, a reputation built over years can be lost overnight.

Priority #5: Thought Leadership

Sharing helpful ideas that deliver value without promoting your product expands your audience, ensuring a steady breadcrumb trail at every stage of the marketing funnel. Remember, at any given time only 5 percent of your buyers are in market; the other 95 percent are not looking for your product or service at the moment. If you give those people useful information, however, they will be more likely to remember you when they're ready to buy.

IMPLEMENTING A GROW WITH TRUST WISH LIST

There are any number of ways to implement Grow With TRUST solutions for your company or clients. What works well for one brand or agency might not work as well for another.

At Idea Grove, we use an approach borrowed from the world of agile software development to guide us.

We call it the Grow With TRUST wish list.

We start with our client's goals. Let's say the client is interested in increasing brand trust through third-party validation, for example.

Working with the client, we brainstorm to identify trust signals that could help achieve this goal. Then, we write down these ideas in a list. A client's wish list might include a wide range of possibilities, such as the following:

- Soliciting more Google reviews
- Getting media coverage for a new product announcement
- Publishing thought leadership articles in *Forbes* or *Fast Company*
- Partnering with top influencers in a new vertical
- Shooting video testimonials to post on the website and share on social media
- Responding to negative Glassdoor reviews
- Earning a Better Business Bureau accreditation
- Applying for an industry award

And many more.

Then comes the hard part. We prioritize which items on the wish list to pursue that month within the program budget.

We look at a number of factors in determining a plan of action:

- Which initiatives should be pursued by the agency team and which by the in-house staff?
- Is timing a factor for some items, such as a product announcement or award deadline?
- Which items can be completed in the upcoming month, and which require a longer-term investment?
- What is the anticipated "bang for the buck" for the different options?

That last question is the most important one of all.

As we discussed in Chapter 8, measuring ROI in branding campaigns is a difficult proposition. But estimating the expected return on competing wish-list items is a far better approach than simply focusing on one tactic at the expense of others or taking a shotgun approach that ultimately has little impact.

Audience research should give a better idea of which trust signals are most important to your buyers and other target groups. Over time, you'll be able to see the impact of your chosen initiatives through measures such as branded search traffic, media visibility, share of voice, review site referral traffic, and social media engagement.

You can follow that up periodically with market surveys and qualitative research.

THE TRUST IMPERATIVE

Securing trust at scale should be every PR firm's business imperative. Because nothing is more important for agency clients today. And no weapon should be left out of the arsenal in pursuit of this goal.

Unfortunately, most of what PR practitioners do today, besides media relations, is viewed as marketing, not PR, by clients.

PR agencies often fail to make a compelling case for why a client should choose them for services such as website design or content strategy. This hinders their growth, because unless they can convince the client otherwise, that client might decide to go with an agency specializing in design or content.

The Grow With TRUST system solves this problem by creating a PR-centric model for brand building in a post-truth world.

It's also the best way for virtually any company to build, grow, and protect its brand.

Conclusion

The New PR: Securing Trust at Scale

Our trust issues didn't begin with the internet.

The quest for trust didn't even start with the first humans 300,000 years ago, according to evolutionary biologists. Trust is a primal need that predates us as a species.

Research of primates, in fact, demonstrates that their capacity to trust is similar to our own. It is an essential glue for their communities.

A UCLA study of capuchin monkeys—popularly known as the favored sidekick of organ grinders—showed that the monkeys go through a fascinating ritual of poking each other in the eye before participating in shared activities, such as hunting.

In his thought-provoking book *The Age of Empathy*, primatologist Frans de Waal referred to this practice as a capuchin "trust fall" (Boser 2014).

The first human societies came together because of trust. The greatest empires endured because of it. And nearly every civilization that has fallen saw the bonds of trust fragment first.

THE MYTH OF THE TRUST DEFICIT

The lack of trust, or at least a necessary level of trust for healthy and sustainable relationships, has come to be characterized in recent years as a *trust deficit*.

I am not a fan of the term because "deficit" means *deficiency in amount*. I would argue—and I think *Trust Signals* demonstrates—that most of us do not have a deficit of trust in our daily lives.

We have, instead, a *displacement of trust*.

We still have trust to give. But we have been forced to reconsider where to invest that trust, and who is worthy of it.

I'm reminded of the poignant line in Paul Thomas Anderson's film *Magnolia*, when the lovelorn and depressed character Quiz Kid Donnie Smith exclaims in desperation: "I really do have love to give. I just don't know where to put it!"

We *must* find places to put our trust in our everyday lives—and we seek out trust signals to find those places.

TRUST SIGNALS AND GROW WITH TRUST

While trust signals have been around since the Pharos of Alexandria and before, in current digital marketing parlance, a trust signal can fall into three categories:

1. **Website trust signals** that encourage visitors to complete a purchase or take an action
2. **Inbound trust signals** that drive visitors to your website via inbound marketing
3. **SEO trust signals** that visitors might not notice, but that Google uses to rank you in search

We introduced these three types of trust signals in Chapters 3–7 of this book. Then, in Chapters 10–15, we explained how these signals could be integrated into a PR system called Grow With TRUST, featuring the following solutions:

- Third-party validation—because people believe what other people say about you more than what you say about yourself
- Reputation management—because a reputation that's worth building is worth defending
- User experience—because how you present your brand across owned media must be consistent to earn trust
- Search presence—because Google is the ultimate arbiter of visibility and trust on the web
- Thought leadership—because 95 percent of your buyers aren't looking to buy right now; share helpful information so they'll remember you when they are

A NEW DEFINITION FOR PR

In addition to introducing trust signals and the Grow With TRUST system, we've covered some other important topics:

- Why the PR profession has declined in influence—and how the Grow With TRUST system can bring it back (Intro and Chapter 1)
- The importance of identifying your brand's target audiences —and how to go about it (Chapters 2 and 9)
- When and how to measure the impact of trust signals on brand building and business growth (Chapter 8)

- How to get started with the Grow With TRUST system (Chapter 16)

Finally, I've introduced a new definition for PR, providing a clear path to meaningfully differentiate our profession:

PR is the art of securing trust at scale.

My deepest wish for this book is that it will encourage other PR practitioners to step into the role of trust expert and advocate for their companies or clients—and that more of my peers and colleagues will begin to view themselves as the keepers of trust for brands.

I urge them to join me in mastering and deploying an evolving set of practices—trust signals—to secure audience trust.

LET TRUST SIGNALS GUIDE YOUR WAY

Today, the United States suffers from a lack of trust in shared institutions like the government, police, and the media.

But we still trust that our electricity will work if we pay our bills on time. We trust that our car's brakes will function at the next red light or stop sign. We trust the people we know we can count on, like friends and family.

And we trust the sources of information in our individual continuums of influence as well.

Trust fragmentation in our post-truth world has resulted in dysfunction in Washington, bitter arguments across social media, conspiracy theories, cancel culture, and more.

But it has also given brands an opportunity to step into the void. Business is America's most trusted institution today, which is why so many consumers look to CEOs to share a vision not just for selling products, but for making the world a better place.

Ultimately, it's a question of supply and demand:

People demand places to put their trust.

Supply them that place and you've got a customer, employee, or fan of your brand for life.

When you build a trustworthy brand, you are doing more than attracting new customers and growing your business. You are helping create a more trustworthy world.

Let trust signals guide your way.

References

Anderson, Chris. 2004. "The Long Tail." *Wired*. October 1, 2004. https://www
.wired.com/2004/10/tail/.

Baymard Institute. n.d. Home page. Accessed August 17, 2022. https://baymard
.com/.

BBB Serving the Heart of Texas. 2021. "BBB Serving the Heart of Texas: 2022
Torch Awards for Ethics." Better Business Bureau. October 6, 2021. https://
www.bbb.org/article/news-releases/25996-2022-torch-awards-for-ethics.

Bernays, Edward. 1928. *Propaganda*. New York: Ig Publishing.

Better Business Bureau. n.d. "Get Accredited." Accessed August 17, 2022. https://
www.bbb.org/get-accredited.

Bhambhri, Anjul. 2012. "Looking for Data Scientists from Within—Start with
Marketing." Dataversity. July 25, 2012. https://www.dataversity.net/looking
-for-data-scientists-from-within-start-with-marketing/.

Blumenthal, Mike. 2019. "Does Review Gating Impact Star-Ratings?" *GatherUp*
(blog). October 17, 2019. https://gatherup.com/blog/does-review-gating
-impact-star-ratings/.

Boser, Ulrich. 2014. "What a Monkey Can Teach Us About Social Trust." *Psychology Today*. September 3, 2014. https://www.psychologytoday.com/us/blog
/the-social-trust/201409/what-monkey-can-teach-us-about-social-trust.

Casado-Aranda, Luis-Alberto, Angelika Dimoka, and Juan Sánchez-Fernández.
2019. "Consumer Processing of Online Trust Signals: A Neuroimaging
Study." *Journal of Interactive Marketing* 47 (August): 159–80. https://doi.org
/10.1016/j.intmar.2019.02.006.

Connell, Adam. 2022. "37 Latest Blogging Statistics, Trends, and Facts for 2022."
Blogging Wizard (blog). June 8, 2022. https://bloggingwizard.com/blogging
-statistics/.

Cutts, Matt. 2010. "How Does Google Determine Domain Age, and Is It Important for Ranking?" Google Search Central. October 26, 2010. YouTube video.
3:19. https://www.youtube.com/watch?v=-pnpg00FWJY.

Cutts, Matt. 2014. "The Decay and Fall of Guest Blogging for SEO." *Matt Cutts*
(blog). January 20, 2014. https://www.mattcutts.com/blog/guest-blogging/.

Dean, Brian. 2021. "Google's 200 Ranking Factors: The Complete List." *Backlinko*
(blog). October 10, 2021. https://backlinko.com/google-ranking-factors.

Deloitte. 2020. "Connecting with Meaning: Hyper-Personalizing the Customer Experience Using Data, Analytics, and AI." https://www.google.com/url?q=https://
www2.deloitte.com/content/dam/Deloitte/ca/Documents/deloitte-analytics
/ca-en-omnia-ai-marketing-pov-fin-jun24-aoda.pdf&sa=D&source=docs&
ust=1660837327951891&usg=AOvVaw07xRbNZCNcsN0xbIcBO6Re.

Eadicicco, Lisa. 2014. "11 Influential Quotes from Google's Sergey Brin, Who Co-
Founded One of the Most Powerful Companies in the World." *Insider*. July 23,
2014. https://www.businessinsider.com/best-quotes-google-sergey-brin-2014-7.

Edelman. 2019. "2020 B2B Thought Leadership Impact Study." November 14,
2019. https://www.edelman.com/research/2020-b2b-thought-leadership
-impact-study.

Edelman. 2021. "Edelman Launches the Edelman Trust Institute." June 3, 2021.
https://www.edelman.com/news-awards/trust-institute.

Edelman. 2022. "2022 Edelman Trust Barometer." https://www.edelman.com/trust
/2022-trust-barometer.

Google. 2022. "Search Quality Evaluator Guidelines." July 28, 2022. https://static
.googleusercontent.com/media/guidelines.raterhub.com/en//searchquality
evaluatorguidelines.pdf.

Google. n.d. "How Search Works: Ranking Results." Accessed August 18, 2o22.
https://www.google.com/search/howsearchworks/how-search-works/ranking
-results/.

Kaley, Anna, and Jakob Nielsen. 2019. "'About Us' Information on Websites."
Nielsen Norman Group. May 26, 2019. https://www.nngroup.com/articles
/about-us-information-on-websites/.

Kessler, Glenn, Salvador Rizzo, and Meg Kelly. 2021. "Trump's False or Misleading
Claims Total 30,573 Over 4 Years." *The Washington Post*. January 24, 2021.
https://www.washingtonpost.com/politics/2021/01/24/trumps-false-or-
misleading-claims-total-30573-over-four-years/.